ELECTIONAL
ASTROLOGY

ABOUT THE AUTHOR

Joann Hampar (New York), a professional astrologer for almost twenty years, attended the American School of Astrology in Manhattan and is certified in both horary and electional astrology. She was a staff writer for *American Astrology* and has contributed to *Dell Horoscope, The Mountain Astrologer,* and Llewellyn's *New Worlds.* Joann resides in Manhattan and Montauk, New York, with her husband of eighteen years and their cat.

JOANN HAMPAR

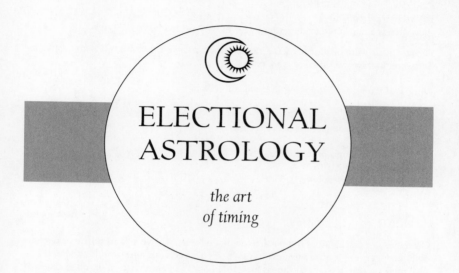

ELECTIONAL ASTROLOGY

*the art
of timing*

Llewellyn Publications
St. Paul, Minnesota

First Edition
First Printing, 2005

Book design by Donna Burch
Cover design by Ellen Dahl
Edited by Andrea Neff
Llewellyn is a registered trademark of Llewellyn Worldwide, Ltd.

Chart wheels were produced by the Kepler program by permission of Cosmic Patterns Software, Inc. (www.AstroSoftware.com).

Library of Congress Cataloging-in-Publication Data

Hampar, Joann.
    Electional astrology : the art of timing / by Joann Hampar.—1st ed.
        p.   cm.
    Includes bibliographical references.
    ISBN 10: 0-7387-0701-5
        1. Electional astrology. I. Title.

BF1717.25.H36 2005
133.5—dc22   2004064961

Llewellyn Worldwide does not participate in, endorse, or have any authority or responsibility concerning private business transactions between our authors and the public.
    All mail addressed to the author is forwarded but the publisher cannot, unless specifically instructed by the author, give out an address or phone number.
    Any Internet references contained in this work are current at publication time, but the publisher cannot guarantee that a specific location will continue to be maintained. Please refer to the publisher's website for links to authors' websites and other sources.

Llewellyn Publications
A Division of Llewellyn Worldwide, Ltd.
P.O. Box 64383, Dept. 0-7387-0701-5
St. Paul, MN 55164-0383, U.S.A.
www.llewellyn.com

Printed in the United States of America

OTHER BOOKS BY JOANN HAMPAR

How to Read Your Birth Chart

(American Federation of Astrologers, 1993)

ACKNOWLEDGMENTS

I would like to thank Stephanie Clement, whose support and input were invaluable to me and helped this book to reach its fulfillment, and Andrea Neff, whose queries and commentary enhanced its content.

DEDICATION

To my friends, you know who you are, whose support and encouragement facilitated my journey on this path.

CONTENTS

CHARTS

This time, like all times, is a very good one,
if we but know what to do with it.

—Ralph Waldo Emerson

chapter one

INTRODUCTION: GENERAL RULES IN ELECTIONAL ASTROLOGY

Electional astrology is utilized in choosing the most appropriate time to begin something. The intent is to achieve a successful outcome, and the rules applied are very specifically set toward that end. Many of the rules have their foundation in horary astrology, the counterpart to this work. Horary astrology is the art of answering a question by analysis of a chart drawn for the precise moment at which the question is asked. Within the horary chart lies the answer to the question, and all circumstances surrounding the matter. Unlike horary, which answers after the fact, electional astrology approaches the matter beforehand and "elects" an appropriate time to achieve a desired outcome. Though the rules are the same, they are applied differently.

The election chart itself is drawn for the place where the event will occur at a certain time in the future. At its best, an election chart will make use of the most beneficial planetary alignments on any given day.

Since the Moon is of primary importance in all election work, she is given precedence, though the rulers of the elected matter are also considered. The Moon's applying aspects describe the unfolding of the electional matter. The Sun and Moon in good alignment will always enhance the election, and contribute to a successful outcome.

The *elected time* is the exact moment chosen to begin something. It is calculated to give you an advantage in the matter. The time selected has a twofold purpose. The primary reason is to strengthen the person initiating the action. This person is always shown by the first house, and the Moon. The secondary reason is to strengthen the house of the electional matter. The house is determined by the main theme of the election. In considering the correct time, one must keep in mind the moment of *finality*. This is when there is no longer any control in the matter, and it is out of your hands. The statement "I now pronounce you man and wife," at the conclusion of a marriage ceremony, is an example of finality. The election time should correspond with the pronouncement, and not with the beginning of the ceremony. Up until that moment, either party can back out. If signing important documents to be returned by mail, finality occurs when the papers are dropped into the mailbox. Until they have left your possession, there is still control in the matter. It is not always easy to determine the moment of finality, so a good rule of thumb is to recognize when something is no longer within your control. Often it is when you have taken the first step to set the matter in motion, but not always.

Both the *natural ruler* and the *natal ruler* of the election matter are considered in setting up an election chart. However, the natural ruler is the primary consideration. The natural ruler is the planet corresponding with the subject of the election. For example, every election pertaining to marriage, or relationship matters, should feature a strong and well-placed Venus. This is the primary consideration, although the natal ruler of the seventh house is also considered. Ideally, an election for marriage would feature a strong Venus, a healthy Moon, and favorable aspects to the ruler of the natal seventh house. Likewise, the signing of important papers requires a sound Mercury. Business matters benefit when Saturn, Jupiter, and the Sun are well aligned. It is always beneficial to strengthen the natural rulers of an electional matter.

The next consideration is the house ruling the electional matter. This is the house corresponding with the main theme of the election. It is necessary to strengthen the *house of the matter,* and link it favorably with the first house. The seventh house is the house of marriage, and the tenth, the house of business. In a marriage election, we want positive aspects between the rulers of the first and seventh houses. In a business election, positive aspects between the rulers of the first and tenth houses are needed.

We can begin by looking for days with positive aspects between the Moon and the planet ruling the electional matter. Only *applying aspects* are considered in electional astrology, as once an aspect is separating, the opportunity is over. The Moon is allowed all applying aspects until she leaves the sign she is in. In other words, the Moon is not confined to an orb of influence. Each applying aspect will describe something about the unfolding of the electional matter. The *final* aspect of the Moon shows the outcome of the election, and is a major consideration. A positive last aspect is very important if the elected matter is to end well.

To a great extent, electional work is subject to certain time constraints. Therefore, it is vital to fortify the Moon. Begin by looking for days when she is making mostly positive aspects. Her *waxing* phase favors growth, and she should be strong by sign, and ideally making no difficult aspects to the Sun or to the planet ruling the matter of the election. The Moon's *waning* phase favors consolidation, and is appropriate when bringing matters to completion. The Moon *void-of-course* is to be avoided when selecting an election date. Actions taken when the Moon is void will not turn out as planned. In horary astrology, if a question is posed when the Moon is void-of-course, the astrologer can say that "nothing of consequence will come of the matter." The Moon is making no contact with the planets, and therefore, no action ensues. The same applies to the election chart.

The *Ascendant ruler* should be strong, in good aspect with the Moon and with the planet ruling the electional matter. The first house and its ruling planet always represent the person who initiates the action, and should be free from affliction. It is necessary to have a positive applying aspect between the planet ruling the first-house person and the planet ruling the house of the elected matter. If there is no contact, no action will ensue. The Moon is always a co-ruler of the first-house person, and can be used to connect the two.

Try to keep the difficult planets away from the Ascendant and out of the first quadrant. Difficult planets in the first quadrant can interfere with the momentum of the elected matter. Saturn may cause delay or require tremendous effort to overcome. Uranus usually presents an unexpected problem or a disruptive influence. Neptune may indicate a lack of information, misinformation, or bad judgment. With Pluto, something needs to be eliminated before the matter can proceed.

Also, try to avoid a *retrograde* significator. This is the planet representing any significant person or matter in the election chart. A retrograde condition is weak and may not function well.

The *quality* of the signs on the angles should also favor the election chart. Cardinal signs support quick action and taking the initiative. Fixed signs support endurance. They are particularly desirable for long-term commitments, such as marriage, or for projects where longevity is vital. Mutable signs encourage change, and are helpful when flexibility is needed.

The *Part of Fortune* is considered favorable, especially if placed in the house ruling the matter of the election. It is also helpful when conjunct the Ascendant. It acts like a benefic planet and can play a significant role. However, it is *not* well placed in the eighth or twelfth house, unless your election pertains to one of those houses. In either house it is considered the Part of Misfortune.

The *mutual reception* of two planets enables the respective planets to change signs, and therefore change positions. This occurs when two planets are in each other's signs. The two planets in mutual reception cooperate with one another, and this lends flexibility and versatility to the matter at hand. It is similar to a conjunction in that the two planets work together as one.

The *critical degrees* 0° and 29° should be avoided. An angle or planet in either of these degrees operates at a disadvantage. The person or matter represented is either premature or too late, respectively. The *malefic degrees* should also be avoided. They are 24° Taurus, 29° Taurus, and 19° Scorpio. The person or matter represented by a planet in one of these degrees is unstable.

The *natal* chart of the individual plays a key role in the success of an election. The birth chart will show one's predisposition in all matters, and should support the focus of the election. The birth chart will affirm whether the goal is realistic.

We also examine the current planetary cycles for confirmation that the election is attainable. They will help us determine whether the overall timing is favorable. In particular, we are most interested in the Saturn cycle. Saturn's transits to the natal chart correlate with obstacles in achieving one's goals. If Saturn is making difficult aspects to the Sun, for instance, it can be quite difficult to succeed with business matters. It is certainly easier to have success with electional astrology if the current cycles agree with the intent of the election. However, an election chart does stand on its own, and should always reflect the best time to support the desired outcome.

chapter two

THE NATAL CHART
AND PLANETARY CYCLES

When working with electional astrology, it is beneficial to begin with an examination of the birth chart. We are looking for confirmation that the natal chart supports the undertaking, and that the timing is appropriate for the electional matter. If the birth chart upholds the matter under consideration, it is much easier to have success with electional astrology. An election date cannot work miracles, but it can give you the inside edge. For example, if you are not qualified for the job you're seeking, it is unlikely that you will get it. However, if you are one of three qualified applicants, an election date will give you the advantage. It's like having the deck stacked in your favor.

Moreover, the current planetary cycles will either aid or hinder the overall timing. A good deal depends on how these dynamics are integrated into the experience. The cycles of Jupiter, Saturn, Uranus, Neptune, and Pluto may be in effect for months or even years. Therefore, it is beneficial to understand each of these in relation to your current objective. Pay particular attention when your Sun, Moon, Ascendant, Ascendant ruler, Midheaven, or Midheaven ruler is activated by one of these cycles, as it can be a time of fresh opportunity.

Jupiter making a strong aspect to the natal chart will usually offer a number of benefits or ease of accomplishment in some area. It is often associated with matters of education, and particularly advanced studies. It can be a time of growth in spirituality or one's philosophical views, including religious attitudes. Jupiter's cycles encourage expansion at every level. The downside of a Jupiter cycle is the inclination to become complacent, or even self-indulgent. It is an ideal time, however, to embrace new concepts and to explore unfamiliar territory. Jupiter making a positive aspect to the natal Sun favors elections for travel, business, advertising, publishing, and legal matters.

Saturn making a strong aspect to the natal chart represents a time to accept responsibility. It is usually associated with the need to take a serious look at your life and learn how to better manage some aspect of it. The process can be a difficult one, especially if you are not satisfied with your progress. Anything undertaken during a Saturn cycle will require dedication and hard work. However, whatever is accomplished will endure. Saturn is evenhanded, giving concrete results for the effort expended. The Saturn cycle represents a time in which resolve and self-discipline yield significant results. Saturn making a positive aspect to the natal Sun favors elections pertaining to business matters, real estate, and establishing new foundations.

Uranus making a strong aspect to the natal chart will more than likely introduce something new. Often it is a time to get rid of things, to free yourself up, and to get ready for the excitement to come. Uranus is all about a willingness to experiment, to be creative and, above all, flexible. It frequently introduces an unknown element, and will test your ability to adapt to change. This is a time to remain unfettered, and to embrace the new opportunities coming your way. When Uranus makes a positive aspect to the natal Sun, it favors elections to establish an association, to travel, to experiment with new technologies, and to legislate.

Neptune making a strong aspect to the natal chart is an invitation to embrace the nonmaterial elements of life. It will encourage action for the good of everyone, and not just for personal gain. It can open a door to creativity and spirituality. Over time, it will dissolve barriers and increase consciousness. A Neptune cycle will often require some personal sacrifice. When it is approached in that way, life can be enriched beyond expectation. However, a selfish approach often leads to abusive or addictive behavior. Neptune can inspire you to go beyond your limitations. It is also associated with increased intuition, insight, and artistic creativity. It can be a time of confusion if you are not embracing these concepts. When Neptune makes a positive aspect to the natal Sun, it favors elections to undertake creative and spiritual work, to volunteer your time, and to offer your services.

Pluto making a strong aspect to the natal chart often requires the elimination of something. The idea is to take stock of your life, get rid of what is no longer necessary, and thus make way for something better. Often referred to as the planet of death and rebirth, it may take different forms. During a Pluto transit it is necessary to go to the root of the problem and face it head-on. The reward for this process is a renewed outlook on life. Pluto is also associated with the need to revisit unresolved issues. It can help bring things out into the open. It is always a time when you can take an honest look at your life and make changes. When Pluto makes a positive aspect to the natal Sun, elections involving elective surgery, shared assets, insurance matters, taxes, and investments are often requested.

The planets associated with good luck are the *Sun, Venus,* and *Jupiter.* When they aspect your personal planets, or when they transit through a house, it is generally easier to achieve something positive. The planet *Mars* represents action and is often involved in creating the environment for things to happen. The *Moon* is very important in electional astrology.

She is the closest body to earth, and indicative of how things will progress and eventually culminate. The Moon is always a *co-ruler* of the person initiating the election. *Therefore, the Moon should always be in a positive applying aspect with the planet ruling the matter of the election.*

Mercury, planet of news, information, and agreements, should always be direct in motion on the day selected to initiate something new. The only time a retrograde condition is acceptable is when you are re-working something that has been tried before. In this instance, a willingness to make changes and reorganize your plan is necessary to the success of the undertaking. Moreover, the Moon should be in good aspect to a retrograde Mercury to ensure the best outcome.

THE SATURN CYCLE

Saturn rules time and has always been connected with the need to persevere in the face of adversity. The positive keywords most often linked with a Saturn cycle are patience, resolve, dedication, tenacity, and determination. On the other end of the spectrum, it can be difficult to succeed with something during a stressful Saturn cycle. Saturn's association with delays, obstructions, interference, and obligations can ambush the project. The challenging lessons so often connected with a Saturn transit will take time to integrate. At the onset of a Saturn cycle, you begin to take stock of your life, and by the completion of the cycle, only the most worthy elements of your life remain intact. It is a time to rid yourself of excess baggage, so to speak.

Since the Sun is so important in electional work, in particular with regard to business and career matters, Saturn's transits to the natal Sun should be noted. Further, Saturn's transits to its own natal position should also be given careful consideration. It takes Saturn approximately two-and-a-half years to pass through a sign, and approximately twenty-nine years to go completely around the birth chart. When we begin with its position at birth, Saturn's seven-year cycles mark significant turning points in the life of the individual. At age seven, Saturn squares its natal position; at age fourteen, Saturn opposes its natal position; and at age twenty-one, it again squares that placement.

One of the most important times in anyone's life is when Saturn transits to conjunct its own natal position. Referred to as the *Saturn return,* it marks a period of completion, when whatever has been the focus of your attention for the last twenty-nine years comes to fruition. If you have been living according to your own standards, it may be a time of fulfillment, and looking toward new horizons. More often, however, it is a time to reassess one's life and make a course correction. The Saturn return is always associated with endings. It is a time of maturity, when the interests of youth no longer seem as relevant as they once were. If where you are in your life is where you want to be, the Saturn return marks a time when one door closes and another opens. Otherwise, it can be a time of crisis.

Electional dates are often requested around the time of one's Saturn return, as it marks a period of endings and new beginnings. In my personal experience, as long as Saturn is not also making an adverse aspect to the natal Sun, most elections will succeed. Of course, the subject matter of the election should be evaluated, but overall it is a constructive time to begin a new endeavor.

Saturn's transits to the natal Sun are very important and are most often related to career and business matters, or to one's goals and objectives. Therefore, elections pertaining to these subjects are requested more often under difficult Saturn transits to one's natal chart. When Saturn transits to *conjunct* the natal Sun, it signals a change in career, work, vocation, or one's objectives. It is a point of culmination, and depending upon the efforts made prior to this contact, it can be a time of honors bestowed and recognition given, or a time of endings and loss. On a lighter note, it can be associated with retirement, stepping back from a heavy workload, or taking on new studies. If Saturn is transiting in conjunction with the natal Sun, an election to start a new career, business, or other work-related endeavor will take time to succeed. It will require a great deal of commitment and hard work to get it going, but that doesn't mean it will not succeed. It does mean that there may be many obstacles to overcome, and the astrologer should inform the client accordingly.

When Saturn transits to *oppose* the natal Sun, there are challenges to overcome often associated with others who are not in agreement with you. This can be a difficult time to initiate something new because outside influences seem to thwart your efforts. The opposition of Saturn to the Sun can mark a period of letting go of certain obligations. Often relationships come to an end under this cycle. Most importantly, it signals a time when things have to be brought to conclusion to clear the way for new initiatives.

To a lesser extent, the transiting *squares* of Saturn to the natal Sun are also inhibiting, but they do not prohibit a successful outcome in an electional matter. As always, the astrologer should evaluate the chart in its entirety to determine the overall probabilities. Saturn's first square to the Sun signals a time of further development. Whatever was begun at the time of Saturn's conjunction to the Sun may need to be revisited. Often, the square is more about reaching within and stretching beyond one's self-imposed limitations. It may also signal a need to be more efficient and to curtail expenses. An election undertaken at the time of Saturn's transiting square to the natal Sun may not have the degree of success desired. It may get off to a slow start, or the person may not have the stamina to see it through.

PLANETS THROUGH THE HOUSES

As a planet transits through a house of the birth chart, it activates that area of life experience. The slower-moving planets bring gradual change over a period of time, while the faster planets exert their influence for shorter durations. It is often the case, when working with electional astrology, that an active house in the natal chart will be the focus of the electional matter. For example, when Saturn transits through the seventh house, a relationship becomes more serious. If it has been progressing well, Saturn's effect is to solidify the relationship. I have often noticed Saturn transiting the client's seventh house when a marriage election date is requested.

When the *first house* is activated by transit, something of a personal nature comes to the fore. It may require your individual effort, and this can be a good time to commit to something of particular value to you personally. When this house is activated, you may decide to focus on your physical fitness or change your appearance. It is related to one's physical stamina, and together with the sixth house, defines one's state of health or imbalance. In electional matters, the first house always defines the person initiating the election, and should therefore be strong and free from any affliction. The planet ruling the first house, and the Moon as co-ruler, should always be as strong as possible, and in a favorable applying aspect with the ruler of the elected matter.

A transit through the *second house* spotlights your personal resources, assets, and innate skills. The second house has a lot to do with what you have to offer the world. Though the second house is also associated with your own money, its deeper meaning symbolizes your capacity to apply your inner resources to something of value. This is an excellent time to acquire a new skill or hone your abilities. Your personal bank account may be affected, with money coming in or going out. An election to buy, sell, or exchange money should strengthen this house.

A transit through the *third house* will focus attention on your daily surroundings. It stimulates contact with those in your immediate vicinity, including neighbors and siblings. You may spend more time talking on the phone, and connecting with all the people in your life. It is likely that paperwork, documents, studies, and tests will occupy your time. Since this is the house of mental activity, a transit here can set the timing for an important decision. An election to take a test, make an announcement or speech, sign papers, or mail an important document should strengthen this house.

A transiting planet through the *fourth house* focuses attention on family matters, the home, and one of your parents. This is the house of inner development, so it is a perfect time to reflect on what is important to you. Give attention to your deepest needs, and make whatever shifts you feel are necessary. If interacting with family, you may revisit something from the past. Also the house of endings, the fourth house shows the outcome of your elected endeavor. The focus is on this house in an election to buy or sell property.

The *fifth house* is the natural domain of the Sun and is considered the house of chance, fun, good times, luck, love affairs, pregnancy, and children. Transiting planets through this house may produce a run of good luck, the birth of a child, or a new creative endeavor. This is also the house of monetary gain from real estate, and should be strong in an election to sell a home or property. It is also a primary consideration in gambling elections, pregnancy, and birth.

A transit through the *sixth house* focuses attention on health maintenance, diet, exercise, and health care professionals. The sixth house is also about duty, service, and the things you are required to do, such as your job, work, and all other work-related activities. It describes the office where you work and your co-workers. It is also a primary consideration in the acquisition and care of small animals. An election to begin a new job, interact with co-workers, begin a health care regimen, or acquire a pet should reinforce this house.

A transit through the *seventh house* highlights your marriage, your relationship with a significant other, or a business partnership. This can be a good time to get married or start a partnership. When this house is activated, you may develop an important relationship, or an existing partnership may come under scrutiny. This is the house of interaction with all others, including strangers and people you hardly know. Strengthen the seventh house in an election to reach an agreement with anyone, to marry, or to begin a partnership. In legal matters, the seventh house represents the opponent. In this instance, unless a settlement is preferred, strengthen the first house. Specific rules pertaining to lawsuits are discussed in chapter 5.

When a planet transits through the *eighth house,* we are often dealing with money matters, but on the receiving end. This is the house of resources that come from others, including your spouse or partner. It can be a good time to ask for a loan, financial assistance, or benefits from insurance. Matters pertaining to wills, life insurance, joint bank accounts, and legacies come under the domain of the eighth house. Strengthen this house in an election to secure financial benefits, settle an insurance claim, borrow money, or ask for alimony.

The *ninth house* is associated with good fortune, endowments, and prosperity. It is Jupiter's natural house. When a planet transits here, you may receive an award or sudden windfall. It is also the house of air travel and higher learning. When this house is activated by transit, you may travel, return to school, or discover an interest in spiritual topics. The ninth house has dominion over distant travel, publishing, licensing, attorney's services, certification, and legalization. Enhance the ninth house in an election pertaining to any of these matters.

The *tenth house* is associated with career, vocation, success, business, public recognition, promotion, honors, and personal achievement. This house is also allied with fame, power, and powerful people. When activated by transit, you may associate with those in high places or receive recognition for your efforts. Important people like an employer, chief executive, judge, or superior also come under the domain of the tenth house. An election to achieve success in business, gain recognition, promote your public image, or receive a favorable ruling must reinforce the tenth house. It is always beneficial to link the tenth house with the elected matter because it is the house of success.

A transit through the *eleventh house* brings attention to objectives as they relate to one's wishes, dreams, and desires. A transit through this house can be a time of adjustment, shifting, or letting go of something to allow more freedom in your life. It is the house of circumstances, and is related to surprises or an unexpected turnaround. The eleventh house is also the house of friends, social life, civic groups, and business income. An election for business should include an unafflicted eleventh house as well as a strong tenth house. It is also important to strengthen this house when starting a group or association.

The *twelfth house* is connected with all matters that require solitude, privacy, or a degree of secrecy. A transit here encourages spending time alone. Some beneficial activities include writing, meditation, spiritual practices, and any creative endeavor that requires a quiet setting. This house is also linked with hospitalization, detention, confinement, or other limiting conditions. Therefore, it is best to delay new action when the twelfth house is activated by transit. It is appropriate to clean house, so to speak, and get rid of things. It may be a time to let go of whatever or whoever hinders your lifestyle. An election for surgery involving a hospital stay should feature good alignments between the eighth and twelfth houses. Strengthen the twelfth house in an election to enter the hospital or a rehabilitation facility.

chapter three

PLANET AND HOUSE RULERSHIPS IN ELECTIONAL ASTROLOGY

WHICH PLANET RULES THE ELECTION?

When working with electional astrology, the purpose is to gain an advantage so as to achieve a desired outcome. Therefore, the planets associated with success and with the subject of the election are given precedence over the other planets. They are the Sun, Moon, Venus, Jupiter, and the planet(s) ruling the matter. An election to submit a manuscript for publication would feature a strong Mercury and Jupiter, the planets ruling writing and publishing. There are four points to consider in evaluating a planet's strength: its position by sign, its position by house, its alignment with the other planets, and its momentum (retrograde or direct).

The strength of a planet by sign is shown in the following table of dignities:

Planet	Dignity	Detriment	Exaltation	Fall
Moon	Cancer	Capricorn	Taurus	Scorpio
Mercury	Gemini/Virgo	Sag/Pisces	Aquarius	Leo
Venus	Taurus/Libra	Scorpio/Aries	Pisces	Virgo
Sun	Leo	Aquarius	Aries	Libra
Mars	Aries/Scorpio	Libra/Taurus	Capricorn	Cancer
Jupiter	Sag/Pisces	Gemini/Virgo	Cancer	Capricorn
Saturn	Capr/Aquarius	Cancer/Leo	Libra	Aries
Uranus	Aquarius	Leo	Scorpio	Taurus
Neptune	Pisces	Virgo		
Pluto	Scorpio	Taurus		

Dignity refers to a planet in its own sign. If a planet is dignified, it is strong, and you are better able to control circumstances.

Detriment refers to a planet in the sign opposite the one it rules. It is not as strong as it should be, and you must compromise or conform to regulations.

Exaltation is the sign in which a planet's strength is magnified. If a planet is exalted, it operates freely and unencumbered.

Fall is the opposite sign of a planet's exalted position, and is a difficult place because it cannot express its real nature.

The strength of a planet by house is also determined by rulership. A planet is strong in its natural house, the house it rules. Mars naturally rules the first house and co-rules the eighth house, and is therefore strong in either house. A planet is also strong in the house ruled by its exalted sign. Therefore, Mars is strong in the tenth house, the house naturally ruled by Capricorn, its sign of exaltation. However, any planet is strong in an angular house (first, fourth, seventh, and tenth) and is described as having *accidental dignity*. The angular houses are considered stronger than succedent or cadent houses, as they are the houses associated with the cardinal points. The cardinal signs take the lead and are action-oriented. Planets in angular houses show immediate action, and bring quicker results in an election chart. The cadent houses (third, sixth, ninth, and twelfth) are considered the least favorable, as they are associated with delay or some hindrance. However, if a planet is naturally strong there, such as Jupiter in the ninth house, it will work well but may result in some delay. Further, if the elected matter is ruled by a cadent house, then strengthen that house.

In electional astrology, it is always advisable to have the planet ruling the matter direct in motion because a retrograde condition weakens and/or delays the outcome. Remember that the condition of any planet is conveyed to the person or matter it rules in the election chart. The aim is to strengthen the planets ruling your election, and connect them in constructive ways.

PRIMARY PLANETARY RULERSHIPS

Planet	Rulership
Sun	Advancement, achievement, one's ambitions, honors, executives, presidents, dignitaries, leaders, bosses, men in general, politicians, promotions, amusements, casinos, resorts, theaters, gamblers, places of entertainment, celebrities, creative endeavors, speculation, children, offspring, one's father. Body part: heart.
Moon	Childbirth, babies, conception, fertility, home, family, property, land, landscapers, one's mother, women in general, the public, public attention, common people, home environment, allergies, boats, boating, fish, fishing, restaurants, food, groceries and grocers, hotels and hotelkeepers, inns, kitchens, collectors, mariners. Body parts: stomach, glandular system.

Planet	*Rulerships*
Mercury	Advertising, agents and agencies, small domestic animals, automobiles and trips by car, bus, or other ground vehicle, books and bookstores, brothers and sisters, relatives, licenses, contracts, documents, reports, educators, elementary school, classmates, all means of communication, employees, laborers, health care practitioners, masseurs. Body part: lungs.
Venus	Actors and actresses, marriage and marriage partner, brides, sweetheart, loves and lovers, money and money lenders, banks and banking, income, alimony, women in general and young women in particular, artists, art dealers and museums, hobbies, parties and celebrations, one's possessions and valuables, music and musicians, jewelry and jewelers. Body parts: throat and neck.
Mars	New ventures, taking action, one's ambitions and initiatives, army and armed forces, athletics and athletes, building and builders, contests and courage, cutting instruments, surgery and surgeons, dentists and dentistry, mechanics and mechanical engineers, males in general, physical therapy and therapists, tournaments, one's sexuality and drive. Body parts: face and head.
Jupiter	Good luck and abundance, bequests and benefits, awards and bonuses, ceremonies, churches and church affairs, long-range advertising, legal matters, legal profession and legalizing, attorneys, courts of law, certificates and certification, credentials, publishing and publicity, copyrights, institutions of higher learning, large animals, air travel and long journeys, priests and clergy, spiritual matters. Body parts: liver and thighs.

Planet	Rulerships

Saturn — Business and places of business, public buildings, foundations, one's profession, career, vocation, employment, bankruptcy, debts and debtors, foreclosures, one's father, elders, enduring friendships, engineers, architects and architecture, building and building materials, landlords, land and property, monks and monasteries, retirement, elders. Body parts: bones and teeth.

Uranus — Divorce, estrangements, earthquakes, hurricanes, accidents, astrology and astrological advisors, broadcasters and broadcasting, radio and television, clubs and clubhouses, airplanes and airports, flying, pilots, electronics and electronic devices, electrical engineers, technology, metaphysics and metaphysicians, telepathy, immigration, science and scientists, animation. Body parts: blood circulation and body's magnetic field.

Neptune — Artistry and artistic taste, artistic genius, music and musicians, dance and dancers, mediums, clairvoyants, one's consciousness, extrasensory perception, cosmic influences, angels, drugs in general, druggists, addictions, the sea, fishing, fishermen and fishing boats, mariners, cameras and photography, charity and charitable institutions, chemistry and chemists, gasoline and gasoline stations, hospitals and hospitalization, floods and places prone to flooding, irrigation, forecasts and forecasting, magic and magicians, mysteries and mystics, navy and naval affairs. Body part: feet.

Pluto — Archeology and archeologists, cemeteries and cemetery workers, coroners and undertakers, cremation, detectives and detection devices, gangsters, life insurance and insurance companies, pensions, pests and pest control, healers and healing without drugs, hidden forces, psychics, psychologists, surgeons and surgery, underground, sewers and septic systems, sexuality and sexual energy. Body parts: reproductive and excretory systems.

WHICH HOUSE RULES THE ELECTION?

The person initiating the action is always ruled by the first house, and the matter under consideration will fall into one of the twelve houses. To work with electional astrology, it is first necessary to identify which of the houses rules the main theme of the election. Although the planets are important, the house ruling the electional matter is the primary consideration. Once the matter has been placed into the appropriate house, we want to arrange the planets to enhance that house.

Selecting the appropriate house is a fairly straightforward matter. The main topic of the election will determine which house applies. However, it becomes a bit more complicated when three or more houses are involved. In that case, we want easy applying aspects between the rulers to bring the matter to a successful conclusion.

In a marriage election, the focus is on strengthening the seventh house. In a business election, the focus is on the tenth house, and in an election to buy property, the fourth house is important. Multiple houses are considered in an election to purchase a home. In such an election, one would consider the fourth house as the primary house because it represents the home. However, the relationship between the first and seventh houses is equally important because they represent the buyer and seller. The second and the eighth houses show their finances. To reach an agreement, we need easy aspects between the first- and seventh-house rulers. Moreover, if the home is to become the property of the buyer, we want to see easy aspects between the rulers of the first, second, and fourth houses as well.

The following section will help you identify where to place the matter. It is always important to connect the rulers of the houses involved by way of positive applying aspects.

First House

The person initiating the election; one's appearance, physical body, physical health; one's carriage, coordination, facial features; one's character, disposition, demeanor, opinion; the impression one makes; one's mannerisms, personality, and temperament.

It is always important to strengthen the first-house ruler and to achieve a favorable applying aspect between that planet and the planet ruling the house of the election. If there is no contact between these planets, no action will occur. The Moon can always be used as a co-ruler of the first-house person, and her applying aspects bring the parties together. The first house is considered in every election, and given special attention in matters pertaining to any personal or physical subject, such as cosmetic surgery, a physical regimen, improving one's appearance, or self-promotion.

Second House

One's money, assets, earnings, and earning capacity; personal finances; material possessions such as jewelry or stocks; one's spending habits, purchasing power, personal debts, personal resources, financial prospects, and financial affairs in general.

The second house is considered in matters pertaining to buying and selling, and whenever money changes hands. Since this is the house of your own personal resources, it is important to strengthen this house when making an investment or purchasing anything for gain, such as stocks, fine jewelry, antiques, or collectibles. Strengthen the second house to increase your earning capacity, improve your credit rating, eliminate personal debt, or borrow money.

Third House

One's decisions, agreements, contracts, and words; tests and examinations; one's early education and teachers; one's way of communicating thoughts and ideas; siblings, neighbors, and one's everyday environment; the neighborhood and travel therein, such as short trips by car, bus, train, bicycle, and other means of transportation.

The third house is considered in all matters where a binding contract or agreement is signed or entered into by mail. It also covers local travel, taking tests, new studies, and schooling. An election to make an important announcement, speech, or declaration should strengthen this house. Former President Ronald Reagan was known to use an electional astrologer to time his important speeches and press conferences.

Fourth House

One's home, family, and domestic affairs; a parent; one's property; land, buildings, real estate, hotels, motels, houses, farms, produce markets, leases, rental property; self-rehabilitation; one's inherited tendencies, ancestry.

The fourth house is considered in elections to purchase a home, a building, property, land, or any real estate. It is also important when renting or leasing property. The fourth house always illustrates the conclusion of the elected matter. It is therefore advantageous to place a benefic planet there whenever possible. The Moon, as the natural ruler of the fourth house, also reflects the outcome of the elected matter. Strengthen this house to buy or rent a home, and to enhance the outcome of your elected matter.

Fifth House

Children, offspring, love affairs, pregnancy; speculation, risk taking, betting, gambling, games of chance, lotteries, raffles; one's artistic and creative endeavors, hobbies, pastimes, enjoyments, and entertainment.

The fifth house is the primary consideration in an election for gambling or any speculative venture where risk taking is involved. This may include casino gambling, lotteries, stock options, the futures market, or the racetrack. An election to begin a new romance would focus on strengthening the fifth house, as would an election to begin a new productive activity. Anything one creates, whether a child, sculpture, or beautiful painting, comes under the auspices of this house. Electional matters involving the welfare of a child would focus on the fifth house.

Sixth House

One's work, voluntary labor; small and domestic animals, pets; one's health care regimen, nutritional preferences, hygiene; healers, occupational therapists; disease, illness; laborers, domestic workers; one's employees, tenants; one's capacity for service.

The sixth house is considered in all matters pertaining to the acquisition or care of pets. It is also the focus of work-related activities, including the hiring of a contractor or other laborer to work for you. Your own voluntary service, such as military service or municipal service, comes under the heading of the sixth house. Your working conditions and interaction with co-workers are shown here. Together with the first house, the sixth house is the main consideration in health-related matters. It is advisable to reinforce this house when undergoing regular health care routines, such as physical examinations and tests, physical therapy, endurance training, and bodybuilding.

Seventh House

Matrimony, marriage both legal and common law, spouse; business partner, business partnerships, alliances; lawsuits, litigation, opponent, rivals, public enemies, strangers, divorce; dealings with the public, one's social functions and social life.

The seventh house is considered when forming any important alliance, such as a marriage or business partnership. To reach an agreement with another individual or group of people, it is necessary to have easy aspects between the rulers of the first and seventh houses. The seventh house is also the focus of litigation, and any interaction with a rival or opponent. If the goal is to achieve a compromise, we would look for positive aspects between the first- and seventh-house rulers. If the intent is to triumph, such as is the case when filing a lawsuit, we would strengthen the first house and link it favorably to the tenth house of judgment.

Eighth House

Alimony, taxes and tax collectors, bankruptcy, finances of one's partner both personal and business; monetary gains from the public, spouse, or business partnership; legacies, inheritances, wills; surgery, surgeons; recovery of a debt, reimbursement of a loss, life insurance, pensions, possessions gained through others.

The eighth house is considered when undergoing any surgery. It is necessary to connect it favorably to the ruler of the first house, and also to the ruler of the twelfth house if the surgery takes place in a hospital setting. The eighth house is also the focus to recover a debt, borrow money, or receive reimbursement through insurance, a tax refund, or other money owed. It is necessary to strengthen this house to file bankruptcy, settle an estate, or obtain public funds. When filing tax returns, strengthen this house and link it favorably with the Moon and the planet ruling the first house.

Ninth House

Advanced education, college, universities, final examinations; legalizing and certifying documents, attorneys and courts of law; publishers and publishing; extended journeys and travel by air; formal ceremonies; advertising that is far-reaching; religion both in practice and the study of philosophical concepts, the clergy, churches, temples, and all other places of worship.

The ninth house is considered when taking a final examination, and in particular one that will result in licensing or certification. It is also the focus to launch a large-scale advertising campaign or to broadcast across the airwaves. In any legal undertaking, the ninth house represents the attorney, and it is necessary to have easy aspects between its ruler and the first-house ruler if the attorney is to succeed for the client. Air travel also comes under the auspices of the ninth house, and a benefic planet here in trine to the Ascendant provides a protective influence.

Tenth House

One's career, profession, vocation, honors and reputation, fame or notoriety, one's business and business affairs; persons in authority including superiors, employers, and judges; officials, important and famous people, one's public image, the dominant parent, one's goals and standing in the community.

The tenth house is the primary focus when a business is launched or if one wishes to embark on a public campaign, such as running for political office. A strong tenth house is necessary to achieve a favorable ruling, judgment, or some type of honor, recognition, or promotion. When beginning a new career, reinforce the tenth house. It is the house of success in all matters. Therefore, depending on the objective of the election, the tenth house and/or its ruler should be well aligned with every other planet in the matter.

Eleventh House

Acquaintances and friends; one's aspirations, hopes, and ideals; finances and income from one's business or profession; civic groups, organizations and club memberships, companions and casual relationships, counselors, fraternities.

The eleventh house is the house of business income, and together with the tenth house should be considered when launching any business or professional endeavor. Ideally, we would like to enhance business income by placing a benefic planet in the eleventh house, or by placing the eleventh-house ruler in the tenth house conjunct a benefic planet. When seeking membership in a club, group, society, or institute, strengthen this house. The eleventh house is considered when forming any alliance involving a group of people or friends.

Twelfth House

Seclusion, charity and charitable institutions, monasteries; confinement of any kind including hospitalization, imprisonment, or institutionalization; confidential matters and activities, hidden things or places, psychic talent and one's capacity to connect with the universal, solitary endeavors such as meditation and spiritual practices.

The twelfth house comes under consideration in an election involving a hospital stay, or entrance into a rehabilitation facility or nursing home. If undergoing surgery, the rulers of the first, eighth, and twelfth houses should be in positive alignment. For all solitary endeavors such as writing or spiritual practices, we would enhance this house. If you want to keep something under wraps, away from prying eyes, or unnoticed, select a time that places the planet ruling the matter in the twelfth house. This can be quite helpful when mailing your tax returns.

IMPROVING HOUSE STRENGTH

There are various ways to strengthen the house ruling the subject of your election. Experience is the best teacher, and the more you work with electional astrology, the better the results. For example, if you were asked to select a favorable date to launch a new business, your focus would be on a strong tenth house. You might choose a time of day when most of the planets are in the Midheaven. If you were unable to achieve that, you might strengthen the planet ruling the Midheaven, and place it in favorable alignment with the Ascendant ruler or the Moon.

Ideally, at least one of the benefic planets should be in a positive aspect with the Moon, or the planet ruling the tenth house, or a planet in the tenth house. It has been my experience that the natural rulers of the matter of the election carry more weight. For example, Venus is the primary consideration in a marriage election no matter what planet rules the election chart's seventh house. The planets of business and success are Saturn, Jupiter, and the Sun. It is important that they be in good aspect to each other and to the Moon, direct in motion, and strong by sign and/or house. In a business election, place Jupiter in the tenth house in good alignment with Saturn and the Sun, or place the planet ruling the business theme in the Midheaven. In an election to open a bookstore, place Mercury in the tenth house.

Try to give priority to the planet ruling the matter, and if possible place it in the house ruling the matter. That planet should be as strong as possible and always in a favorable aspect with the Moon. There are more than a few ways to accomplish what you want. However, the planet ruling the matter of your election should be direct in motion, if possible in the house ruling the matter, in good aspect to the luminaries, and in good aspect to the other planets ruling the matter. The sign the planet occupies is of secondary importance. Since you will seldom be able to achieve an ideal situation, give priority to the Moon. *She should always be in a positive applying aspect with the planet ruling the matter of the election because she is always a co-ruler of the person initiating.* The Moon's applying aspects connect the person with the matter under consideration.

REVIEW

- Look for days with positive transits from one of the fortunate planets to your Sun, Moon, Ascendant, Ascendant ruler, or a planet in your first house. These are days that give you some advantage.

- A positive transit activating the natal house of the matter under consideration can work to your advantage. Use it in combination with an election chart to empower the outcome you want.

- Make certain the planet ruling the matter of the election is direct in motion.

- Identify which house rules the matter of your election.

- Identify which planets rule the subject of the election.

- Look for days when the Moon is strong and free from affliction.

- Look for days when the Moon is in good alignment with the Sun and/or planet(s) ruling the subject of your election.

- Fortify the planetary rulers of the election.

- Fortify the house ruling the election matter.

chapter four

THE MOON IN
ELECTIONAL ASTROLOGY

The Moon is very important in electional work, as she is responsible for setting events in motion, and is always a co-ruler of the election. Her position by sign and relationship with the other planets determines the ease or difficulty with which your elected endeavor will proceed. A primary consideration is her *void-of-course* condition. When the Moon is void, nothing of consequence comes of your election because there is not enough momentum to get it going.

The Moon changes signs approximately every two-and-a-half days, and is void-of-course when she ceases to form any major *applying aspects* to other planets before moving into the next sign. This can occur for a few minutes, a few hours, or longer, depending upon the positions of the other planets. We work with the major Ptolemaic aspects: the conjunction, sextile, trine, square, and opposition. We also consider two minor aspects, the parallel and contraparallel. However, once the last major aspect is formed, the Moon is considered void until it moves into the next sign.

As a general rule, a void-of-course Moon does not favor activities that require mental alertness or concentration. Therefore, try not to schedule anything of importance when the Moon is void. The Moon's lack of contact with the other planets seems to support intuition and perception over intellectual functions. Ordinarily, actions taken during a void-of-course Moon do not turn out as expected. Decisions may never be acted upon, or a project may fail to get off the ground.

Once you have determined the Moon is not void-of-course, you should know two things about the time at which you want to do something: (1) what is the Moon's next applying aspect, and (2) what is the final aspect she makes before changing signs. These two factors describe what to expect initially, and what is likely to be the final outcome.

Because the Moon moves so quickly, she may make several aspects during the course of the day. The Moon's first applying aspect, at the time you begin something, describes how your action gets off the ground or the circumstances you may encounter. The Moon's last aspect before she changes signs describes the end result or eventual outcome of your action. Further, the nature of the planet being aspected by the Moon will tell you something about what you can expect. When the Moon's final aspect is to a *returning retrograde* planet, if favorable, someone returns, or some opportunity reemerges to help you succeed. If the Moon's final aspect is difficult, the person returns to thwart your success, or a troublesome situation reemerges and stops you.

For purposes of determining the best time to initiate an action, the nature of each aspect is as follows:

- The *conjunction* (☌) is usually a favorable aspect. It supports the beginning of something new or the early stages of development. It brings people together. You should initiate action.

- The *sextile* (✶) is a favorable aspect offering opportunity, information, and favorable circumstances. It favors discussion, communication, and information gathering.

- The *square* (□) is a difficult aspect, although it can be overcome with effort on your part. It often requires hard work to get things off the ground.

- The *trine* (△) is a very good aspect and usually requires little effort to get things going. It brings favorable results, often a stroke of luck and foreknowledge.

- The *opposition* (☍) is almost always difficult, but you are fully aware of the problem. You can come to an agreement if you are willing to give up something; otherwise, the matter is dropped.

- The *parallel* (∥) acts like a favorable conjunction in that it brings people together despite their differences. Help comes from someone else. Although it is considered a positive final aspect, it may not be strong enough if the other rulers are hindered.

- The *contraparallel* (#) indicates temporary help to accomplish the matter, such as the aid of an attorney or other professional. As a final aspect, it may not be strong enough if the other rulers are hindered.

An elected date and time should have the Moon making a positive final aspect in addition to having the planets ruling the matter of your election strong and unafflicted. When the Moon makes a final positive aspect to a *retrograde* planet, the matter may still succeed, but you may have to repeat something or make changes. There is the possibility that you will drop the matter altogether. When the Moon's final aspect is a *refranation,* something is dropped and/or someone decides not to follow through and the project is abandoned. A refranation occurs when the Moon is applying to a planet that moves out of the sign it is in before the Moon has a chance to complete the aspect. This will most often occur when a planet is in the last degree of a sign. The Moon cannot make contact before the planet moves into the next sign, and the person or circumstance symbolized by the planet is deserted.

It is best to begin a new project or one that requires growth after a *new* Moon. The two-and-a-half-week period after the new Moon is her *waxing* phase. She is increasing in light, and anything begun during this time has the best chance for growth and expansion. The two-and-a-half-week period after the *full* Moon is her *waning* phase. She is decreasing in light. This is the best time to consolidate, organize, and complete whatever was begun earlier. The *sign* the Moon occupies on any particular day gives a general indication of the mood or disposition of people in general. The Moon sets the tone, and when she passes through an air sign, there is lots of talk but not as much action. When the Moon passes through a fire sign, people are enthusiastic and ready for action. The following table provides a brief description of these indicators.

MOON THROUGH THE SIGNS

- *Aries* favors quick action. When the Moon is here, people are active and energetic, and may be somewhat aggressive and headstrong. Mars is the underlying influence.

- *Taurus* favors a cautious, methodical approach, and when the Moon is in this sign, people are concerned with money and possessions. The Moon is exalted here, and the underlying influence is Venus.

- *Gemini* is a restless sign, and the Moon here is indecisive, often indicating a change in plans or circumstances. It favors doing two things at once. The underlying influence is Mercury.

- The *Cancer* Moon is strong in her own sign and favors nurturing yourself and others. Domestic issues and family matters come to the fore.

- The *Leo* Moon encourages displays of affection and generosity. Gain from taking a risk or chance is favored. The underlying influence is the Sun.

- The *Virgo* Moon is concerned with detail, service, and analysis. When the Moon is here, she favors work and routine tasks. The underlying influence is Mercury.

- *Libra* accentuates teamwork, and the Moon here favors joint projects, marriage, and partnerships. The underlying influence is Venus.

- The *Scorpio* Moon brings out strong passions and desires, and there is something hidden or secretive about the matter. The underlying influence is Pluto.

- *Sagittarius* brings out the desire for adventure, and Moon here favors exploring new ground and a willingness to go beyond your limitations. The underlying influence is Jupiter.

- *Capricorn* is serious, and when the Moon is here, serious work is on everyone's mind. Things proceed more slowly than usual. The underlying influence is Saturn.

- The *Aquarius* Moon favors groups of people getting together, spontaneity, and an unexpected outcome. The underlying influence is Uranus.

- The *Pisces* Moon heightens sensitivity, and people can be distracted. This sign favors spiritual and artistic endeavors. Misunderstandings are common. The underlying influence is Neptune.

If you don't have time to prepare an election chart, you can still work with the Moon's daily motion. Look for a positive applying aspect to begin your project. Then look ahead to the Moon's last aspect, which will tell you the eventual outcome. It doesn't matter how long it takes the Moon to finish making all her aspects. If you begin your activity on

Monday at 11:00 AM, and the Moon is applying to sextile Venus, look ahead to the Moon's last aspect before she changes signs. If the Moon's last aspect is the next day at 2:00 PM, that is still your frame of reference to verify the outcome. Only applying aspects need be considered, and the aspect must be in effect at the time you begin your activity. If you schedule an appointment for 11:00 AM, the first applying aspect is the next one that occurs after that time.

Tracking the Moon's daily activity will enable you to determine the best time to take action. Even on short notice, you can always use the Moon's motion to maximize success.

MORE ABOUT THE MOON

Every aspect the Moon makes has something to say about the unfolding of your electional matter. In electional astrology the primary consideration is the Moon, whereas in natal astrology it is the Sun. This is because the Moon rules all action that will take place, she co-rules the first-house person who initiates the action, and she brings everything together with her applying aspects. Her importance cannot be understated. It is the basis for success with electional astrology. Therefore, keep the Moon strong and free from difficult aspects, and let her apply by favorable aspect to the ruler of the electional matter. In order of importance, the Moon is the primary consideration. The planet that naturally rules the subject of the election and the house ruling the matter of the election are both of equal importance. The angular relationships, or aspects, between the planetary rulers of the electional matter are considered next. The signs the planets occupy and the quality of the signs on the angles are given final consideration.

The Moon's applying aspects describe the action that will take place, while her separating aspects describe what has already taken place. In an election to accomplish something in the future, we are therefore only concerned with her applying aspects. The Moon's first applying aspect tells you how the matter will begin, and every aspect thereafter, how it will progress.

The more applying aspects the Moon makes, the more activity will ensue, and our objective is to avoid many difficult aspects. However, those days when the Moon is completely free from difficult aspects are few and far between. If the Moon applies to a square aspect, it simply means there is some difficulty to overcome. The nature of a square aspect is to provide the impetus to overcome the problem; it does not prevent success. However, the less afflicted the Moon, the better the outcome of your election.

The Moon's final aspect, though, must be a positive one for the matter to end well. And ideally you do not want the Moon's final aspect to be to a retrograde planet, because this can indicate some change in circumstances that leaves you dissatisfied with the outcome. With a positive last aspect to a retrograde planet, you might succeed, but if the planet represented a key person in the matter, that person may change position and leave you somewhat disappointed. A positive last aspect to a retrograde planet need not be detrimental. The election can still succeed, especially if the planet is not a key significator in the election.

The Moon also rules change, and the purpose of an election is usually to alter, modify, or transform something, otherwise we wouldn't be working with electional astrology. Wherever we find the Moon in the election chart, some change will occur. If the Moon is above the horizon, the changes are out in the open and often pubic. Also, if the Moon is in an angular house, she brings attention to the matter.

Because the Moon is a co-ruler of the chart, her quality is revealing. When she is in a cardinal sign, the person initiating has more control of the matter. When she is in a fixed sign, it may take longer to get things going, but it endures. When the Moon is in a mutable sign, there is room for change, if needed. This can be valuable in circumstances where flexibility is key.

The Moon should never be intercepted in an election chart. An intercepted Moon in any house would delay, disrupt, or interfere with the matter. It can mean something is hidden, or the person is unaware of the full scope of the matter. Additionally, the Moon should not be placed in a critical degree (0° or 29°), as this is a weak position for the Moon. It can mean the person is under extreme anxiety, or the situation is desperate.

If the Moon makes an inconjunct (also known as a quincunx aspect), although it is not a major aspect, it is of benefit to consider its meaning in an electional chart. An applying inconjunct aspect indicates the likelihood that something will need to undergo restructuring. If the Moon inconjuncts the Sun, an important person may withdraw his support or abandon the project. If the Moon inconjuncts Mercury, a new broker or agent may enter the picture or papers may have to be redrawn. The Moon quincunx Venus can indicate a change in finances, and quincunx Mars, an adjustment in the overall process. If the Moon inconjuncts Jupiter, the adjustment is beneficial and usually an improvement. The Moon quincunx Saturn may delay the outcome. If the Moon applies to inconjunct Uranus, there may be an unexpected change or a quick resolution to the problem. When the Moon inconjuncts Neptune, something hidden is revealed. If the Moon makes a quincunx to Pluto, there is a secret to be exposed.

When the Moon's final aspect is a trine, the end result is achieved more easily than you anticipated. The area of the election chart ruled by that planet will tell you who or what helped you achieve your objective. When her final aspect is a conjunction, it indicates that the elected matter represents a new beginning, such as a marriage or the purchase of a new home. If the Moon's final aspect is a sextile, the elected matter offers an opportunity to learn something, exchange ideas, or become knowledgeable in some area. The parallel of declination, although considered a minor aspect, is a favorable last aspect when the election chart is strong. The parallel acts as a favorable conjunction, and when the

Moon's last aspect is a parallel to a benefic planet, help comes from the person or thing ruled by that planet. The contraparallel is also an acceptable last aspect, provided the Moon is strong in the election chart. It is indicative of someone or something that provides temporary aid to accomplish the goal, like a realtor who helps close the deal.

SOLAR AND LUNAR ECLIPSES

A *solar* eclipse is when the Moon blocks the Sun's light, thus diminishing its strength. Since the Sun is always important to the success of any elected endeavor, an eclipse can be difficult to recover from. You may lose standing, or someone you were depending upon may disappoint you. An eclipse will often bring something to light, and the more information you have, the better your success with election. What's more, an eclipse always brings an unexpected change in direction, and for this reason it is not the most stable environment in which to launch an election.

If an eclipse happens to aspect your birth chart in a favorable way, it may provide the impetus to accomplish something of importance. More often than not, however, it is best to delay action around the time of an eclipse. There is no hard and fast rule with regard to timing close to an eclipse but a window of up to one week before an eclipse, and one week after the event, should prove satisfactory. An eclipse ushers in changes, and the house axis in which the eclipse takes place will give some indication of where to expect those changes. Moreover, any natal planet aspected by an eclipse will further define what topics you may be dealing with in the months ahead. The orb of influence to natal planets for both solar and lunar eclipses is five degrees.

The effects of a solar eclipse may be felt for up to one year after the event, while the influence of a lunar eclipse may linger for up to six months. The period around a solar eclipse, even up to one month in advance, can be somewhat chaotic because so much is going on. This sense of confusion is a reflection of the changes about to take place. A solar eclipse usually marks the beginning of something new, while a lunar eclipse often brings something to conclusion.

A *lunar* eclipse occurs when the earth is between the Moon and the Sun, obscuring the light of the Sun from the Moon. Lunar eclipses are associated with emotional upsets that may bring something to closure. Therefore, certain events that follow a lunar eclipse can become critical. It can certainly work to your advantage when other planetary influences are supportive. For example, a lunar eclipse can provide the impetus to end a relationship that is no longer wanted. Nevertheless, because of the emotional tone of a lunar eclipse, it's best to delay electional matters. Events that follow an eclipse, solar or lunar, usually carry more weight, and help you make major changes in your life. With a lunar eclipse, you are aware of what needs to be done. Someone may openly oppose your plans or leave you stranded. The sensitive nature of a lunar eclipse can signal a critical situation that needs careful handling. *As a general rule, delay electional matters until at least one week before and after a solar or lunar eclipse.*

OCCULTATIONS

An occultation occurs when the Moon conjuncts a planet and is also eclipsing it by declination. Occultations prevent you from getting the full benefit of the planet occulted. If that planet plays an important role in your elected endeavor, or is the ruling planet of the matter in question, you may not succeed in the way you intended.

When the Moon occults Venus, you do not get the benefits you were expecting. Resources are limited or money is deficient. Certainly you would try to avoid an occultation to Venus if you were choosing a marriage date. If the Moon occults Mercury, you may be missing some important information, and your elected event suffers as a result. The Moon occulting Mars may interfere with your actions and inhibit momentum. The Moon occulting Jupiter lessens the helpful nature of that planet, and whoever or whatever Jupiter represents in your election chart is less effective.

An occultation may work to your advantage if the planet occulted is one of the more troublesome energies, such as Uranus. When the Moon occults Uranus, the unexpected upset or behavior is somewhat muted. However, it goes without saying that if Uranus were a key significator in your election, you would avoid such a condition.

COMBUSTION

This term refers to the first twelve hours after a new Moon, when the Moon is very close to the Sun. At this time the Moon is said to be *combust,* or burned up by the Sun's rays, weakening her strength. Though it is best to begin most projects after a new Moon, the first twelve hours should be avoided.

A planet can also be combust the Sun, and is considered burned up by the Sun's rays if within eight degrees of the star. This position weakens the strength of the planet, and renders it unable to function to its fullest potential. The only *exception* to this rule is the fire planet Mars, considered very strong when conjunct the Sun. In my personal experience, Mars in this position operates without interference, and when well aligned with the other significators, assures the success of the election.

REVIEW

- Choose a positive applying aspect at the time you begin your activity.
- Consider only the Moon's applying aspects.
- Avoid the times when the Moon is void-of-course.
- Keep the Moon as free from difficult aspects as possible.
- For long-term projects, choose a waxing Moon.

- The Moon's final aspect should always be positive.

- Avoid elections around solar or lunar eclipses.

- Consider occultations and combustion.

chapter five

ELECTIONS FOR
EVERY OCCASION

Most people turn to an electional astrologer when planning an important event, such as a marriage or the launching of a new business venture. Yet, electional astrology can be used for anything where a positive outcome is desired. An election chart is simply an event chart in which you predetermine the date and time that will best support the outcome you want. Once you become familiar with electional astrology, you will want to use it all the time. After all, your time is valuable, so why not get the results you want every time?

An election can be used just as easily for more mundane matters, such as a visit to the dentist, as for more important events. In every election chart, more than one house is involved because the subject of the election encompasses several areas. However, there is always one primary house to consider, and the main theme of the election will help you determine which house applies. In the following section, I have included election charts dealing with some ordinary topics to illustrate how easy it is to use electional astrology for just about anything.

FIRST-HOUSE ELECTIONS

Matters that come under the first house include any change in physical appearance, such as to one's hair, face, and body, or a personal coming out, such as a television interview, presentation, stage appearance, or public speech. The first house is important in any election as it always represents the person initiating the action, but it is given added consideration when the focus is on a very personal, individual accomplishment.

Election for an Audition

Going to an audition for a part in a play, movie, or stage performance falls under the domain of the first house together with the fifth house of one's talents. The natural ruler of the first house is Mars, providing the necessary drive in matters of a highly personal nature. One's talents fall into the fifth house, naturally ruled by the Sun. The seventh house is also considered as it rules all others with whom the applicant will meet. They are strangers who will decide whether or not the audition merits further consideration.

If possible, the natural rulers of the matter, Mars, Venus, the Sun, and the Moon (co-ruler of the first-house person) should be well aligned with each other. It is advantageous to have the Moon in Leo, the sign of celebrity, and/or to place Leo on the Ascendant for added recognition. The main objective in this instance is to bring attention to the personal first house, and to make a flattering impression. Therefore, we want to reinforce the first house in any way we can. If possible, place Venus, the Sun, or Jupiter in the first house and well aligned to the other rulers, or place the ruler of the first in the fifth house trine the Ascendant. The Moon is always a co-ruler of the first-house person, and should apply favorably to the rulers of the fifth and seventh houses. Because the Moon moves so fast, it is always possible to use her in favor-

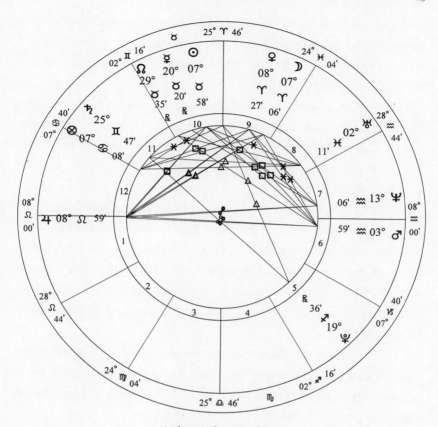

Audition Election Chart
April 28, 2003 / 12:06:35 PM EDT / Manhattan, New York
Placidus Houses

able applying aspect with the other house rulers to bring the matter to a favorable conclusion. Work with whatever favorable alignments you have on any given day. If the Moon is trine the Sun, make those luminaries the rulers of your election.

In every election, the tenth house represents success. In matters of a personal nature, if you are unable to bring all the elements into play, concentrate on easy applying aspects between the Moon or the planet ruling the first house, and the planet ruling the tenth house of success. Make certain that the Moon's final aspect is a positive one. It is always advisable to keep the difficult planets out of the first quadrant, and even more so in matters of a very personal nature, such as an audition. The logic behind this rule stems from the premise that the election chart is not static but continues to reflect the evolution of the matter. Therefore, as the Ascendant progresses to conjunct planets in any of the first three houses, one may expect a corresponding encounter as described by that planet.

The end of the matter is always shown by the fourth house in the election chart. It should confirm the outcome described by the other significators and the Moon. Examine the planet ruling the fourth house and/or any planet in that house for confirmation.

An aspiring actress asked me to select a date and time for her to answer a casting call. This election is very much a personal endeavor in which the objective is to make a strong first impression, and to get the part. Therefore, the first house is key. In this instance, the significant time is when she leaves her apartment to begin her quest, because there were many people auditioning for the part in this stage production, and she was unable to control the surrounding circumstances. Although she would get a late start, I preferred to select a time that allowed Leo to be on the Ascendant with the Sun, her ruler, positioned in the tenth house of success. The interception of the Sun is not necessarily a disadvantage, although it does imply a delay in the matter. As we will see, it turned out that way.

The primary significators of this election are the Sun and Moon, ruling the client; Jupiter and Pluto, ruling her fifth house of talent; Uranus, Saturn, and Neptune, ruling the seventh house of others; and Mars and Venus, ruling the tenth house of success. Jupiter conjunct the Ascendant would certainly give her an edge, but even more so because it rules the election fifth house of her talents. It also co-rules the ninth house of luck and faith. This placement will bring immediate recognition of her exceptional talent.

The Moon's first applying aspect is a conjunction with Venus, one of the tenth-house rulers. This is a very good indication that she will immediately gain the attention of someone in a position of authority. Venus is also the natural ruler of one's talents, so we can conclude that her talents will impress them. The Moon will next trine Jupiter, ruling the fifth house of her talents and co-ruling the election ninth house. The Moon will then sextile Neptune, a co-ruler of the seventh house of others. This aspect confirms a favorable response from the strangers who may judge her. Neptune is the natural ruler of dance, and among her many talents, she would employ her dance skills for this part.

The Moon will lastly sextile Saturn, another co-ruler of the seventh house. Saturn is also the natural ruler of the tenth house of success. This last aspect is confirmation enough of a favorable outcome. However, we look to the end-of-the-matter fourth house for further confirmation of a favorable outcome. It is ruled by Venus; the Moon applying to conjunct her confirms the outcome we want.

As mentioned, the Sun in fixed Taurus is intercepted in the tenth house. However, the Sun is determined in the sign of Taurus, and it symbolizes her resolve in pursuing the part. She was asked to come back several times before a decision was reached. The fixed angles were also supportive in helping her stick with the process. Once things got underway, there was no stopping her. She did indeed get the part, although it took several weeks of going back and forth before the decision was made.

Election for Cosmetic Surgery

An election for cosmetic surgery, in particular when it involves the face, is placed in the first house and, together with the eighth house of surgery, is the primary consideration because the patient is most important. Elective surgery, as opposed to emergency surgery, usually allows the participant to select the date and time, and only in this instance is an electional chart appropriate. Even under these circumstances, it is important to clarify whether the doctor performing the surgery will cooperate with you in beginning at the designated time. This type of election is often done for someone undergoing surgery in the doctor's office. Cosmetic procedures and dental surgery most often fall into this category. Here is where you have the most control in setting the event in motion.

As already stated, the first house is the primary focus when considering facial surgery, and together with the eighth house, the first house should be strong. Surgery and surgeons fall under the rulership of Mars and the eighth house. Cosmetic procedures fall under the rulership of Venus. Dental surgery should include good aspects to Saturn. Therefore, Mars, Venus, and the ruler of the first house should be in harmonious alignment. The Sun is also very important as it adds protection and strength. Try to have the Sun well aligned with the Ascendant, or the Ascendant ruler and the Moon. If the natural rulers of any matter are not cooperating, you would always make use of whatever planets are well aligned and make sure the Moon is favorable to these.

Additionally, the Moon should not be in the sign ruling the part of the body to undergo surgery. Ideally, the Moon should not apply to a difficult aspect with the Ascendant or any planet, but especially not with the malefics. And all surgery should be avoided at the time of the full Moon. Since the Moon is a co-ruler of the person initiating action, she should always apply to a favorable aspect with the ruler of the house in question.

The Moon's applying aspects always describe the unfolding of the event from beginning to end. To ensure a successful surgery, try to select a day when the Moon is making only positive aspects. Listed here are some of the sign rulerships relative to surgery:

Sign	Part of the Body
Aries	Head, face
Taurus	Throat, neck
Gemini	Hands, arms, shoulders
Cancer	Breasts, stomach
Leo	Back and sides of the body
Virgo	Solar plexus
Libra	Lower back, buttocks
Scorpio*	Reproductive system
Sagittarius	Hips, thighs
Capricorn	Skin, teeth, lower legs
Aquarius	Varicose veins
Pisces	Feet, toes

*Moon in Scorpio is considered unfavorable for any kind of surgery.

A retrograde Mercury is clearly undesirable for surgery, and would likely result in the need for a second procedure. You would also avoid retrograde Mars and Venus. In any election, the natural rulers of the elected matter should be direct in motion. Even if you are not able to make use of a natural ruler, it still carries weight.

Try to keep the difficult planets out of the first quadrant, and especially the first house. Jupiter, Venus, and/or the Sun on the Ascendant is always beneficial and protective. If possible, place one of the benefic planets or the Part of Fortune in the eighth house in trine to the Ascendant. One way this can be accomplished is by manipulating the wheel to duplicate the cusp signs. This is simply a matter of changing the time

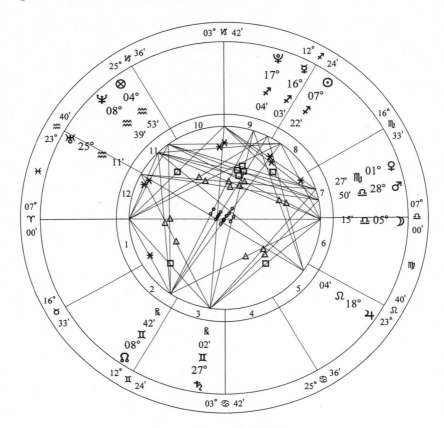

Cosmetic Surgery Election Chart
November 29, 2002 / 1:38:09 PM EST / Manhattan, New York
Placidus Houses

(the Ascendant moves forward at the rate of one degree every four minutes). The objective is to strengthen the first house of the physical body. We also want the planet ruling the surgery, the Moon, and the Ascendant or its ruler in a favorable alignment.

When you are not able to set the time for elective surgery, select a day when the Moon is making only positive aspects and is not in a sign ruling the part of the body to undergo surgery. Mars should be strong and in good alignment with the Moon. Ideally, Mars should be free from any difficult aspects, but mainly avoid those to Saturn, Uranus, Neptune, and Pluto.

The client assured me that her surgeon was willing to begin the procedure at the time selected. It was to take place in the doctor's office, and included lip enhancement and the removal of excess skin under the eyes. Aries, ruling the Ascendant, represents my client, so Mars and the Moon are her significators. The surgery and the surgeon are ruled by Mars and Pluto, and co-ruled by the Sun posited in the eighth house. Since Mars is the primary ruler of the Ascendant, we use Pluto and the Sun for the surgeon. The Ascendant will apply to trine both the Sun and Pluto, a good indication that the surgeon will satisfy his patient and accomplish the task with ease.

Adding to the benefit of this election is the conjunction of Mars and Venus, also in mutual reception. Since they are the natural rulers of surgery and beauty, and are in mutual reception, we can conclude that the client will regain her youthful appearance. They also rule the election first and seventh houses, so the client and all others she may encounter in this process will work well together.

The Moon in Libra is quite favorable for any cosmetic procedure because it is disposed by Venus. Her first applying aspect is a sextile to the Sun in the eighth house of surgery. This is a pretty good indication that the procedure will begin well. The Sun in Jupiter's sign describes the surgeon as a specialist in his field. The Sun and Jupiter are also in mutual reception, attesting to both the excellent reputation of the surgeon and the quality of care. By way of reception, both planets are trine the Ascendant, lending a protective influence. The mutual reception enables the respective planets to change signs, and therefore change positions. So we can conclude that the surgeon is very capable, has a good deal of latitude, and can manipulate circumstances to accomplish what he wants.

The Moon's next aspect, a trine to Neptune, the natural ruler of eyes, is supportive. In fact, all of her applying aspects are favorable, and her final aspect, a conjunction to Mars, adds to the positive nature of this election. We can say the end result will be the start of a new phase for her. Once again, we look to the end-of-the-matter fourth house for confirmation of the outcome. The Moon rules the end of the matter, giving us the corroboration we want. The cardinal angles, as well as the Moon in cardinal Libra, supported an expeditious process and a speedy recovery. Shortly after her surgery, she called to tell me she was very happy with the results and felt better than she had in years.

SECOND-HOUSE ELECTIONS

The second house is considered in elections to acquire valuables such as jewelry, art, equipment, or stocks. It is also the main focus to borrow money, together with the eighth house of money received from others. The second- and eighth-house axis is involved with buying and selling, representing your assets and those of the other party, respectively. The natural rulers of these houses, Mars and Venus, should be as strong as possible in any election involving the exchange of money. The seventh house represents the other party in the transaction. To buy property, consider the second house together with the fourth. To buy speculative stocks, consider the second house together with the fifth.

Election to Purchase Jewelry

The second house is considered when making any purchase. The purchase becomes final when the money exchanges hands. When purchasing

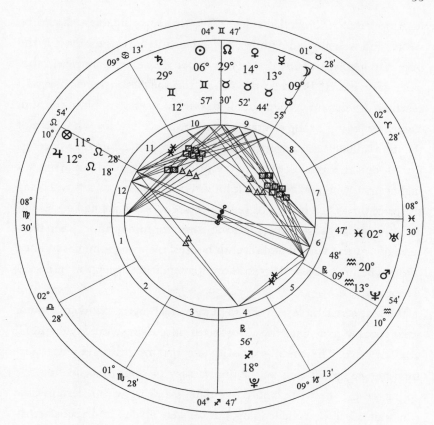

Purchase Diamond Election Chart

May 28, 2003 / 12:44 PM EDT / Manhattan, New York

Placidus Houses

jewelry, Venus, the natural ruler of jewelry and valuables, should be strong and well aligned with the Ascendant ruler and the Moon. If the purchase involves a private party, consider the seventh house. In that case, easy aspects between the rulers and the Moon is necessary to reach an agreement. When adding to one's possessions, place the Sun, Venus, or Jupiter in the election second house to improve the value of the item and ensure its worth. To get the best value, buy on a decreasing Moon, as it tends to lower the price of your purchase. To get a higher price when selling, choose an increasing Moon, as this will bring the price up. When buying or selling, the Moon well aligned with Mercury is a plus because you want trouble-free communication. Keep Neptune out of the second and seventh houses. Neptune, often associated with some pretense or exaggeration, may indicate deception or an unfair price.

Here is an example of a not-so-perfect election that worked because we were able to achieve the objective of purchasing a quality diamond at a fair price. The client wanted to surprise his girlfriend with a diamond engagement ring on the anniversary of their first meeting. He contacted me the week before that date. Working within certain time constraints is always challenging, but we were able to find a satisfactory date.

Virgo on the Ascendant allows Mercury and the Moon to rule the client. He is purchasing, so the second house and Venus describe his resources and the valuable jewelry he is acquiring. Venus, dignified in its own sign, indicates that the client has ample resources and is willing to make a considerable expenditure. It also shows his desire to acquire a fine-quality diamond. Both the Moon and Venus are strong: they are posited in the fortunate ninth house, and the Moon is exalted in Taurus, while Venus is dignified there.

Both significators place the client in a stronger position than the merchant. The merchant is shown by the seventh house ruled by retrograde Neptune. The seventh house is co-ruled by Jupiter, and in the end, would prove to be the saving grace. Though the Moon would apply to square Neptune, an indication of some deception, her final aspect was a parallel to Jupiter. This would prove to be enough to overcome the Moon's square aspects to Neptune and Mars. Interestingly, both planets correctly described what took place during the transaction. The merchant was not quite truthful in that he misrepresented the rating of the diamond. Neptune ruling the seventh house warned of just such a possibility. However, the client was forewarned and insisted on obtaining an independent appraisal before making the purchase. Further, Neptune retrograde hinted at the possibility that the merchant's position was weak.

The Moon next conjuncts Mercury, ruler of the client and the tenth house of success. She next conjuncts Venus, so we can conclude that the client would find a diamond he wished to purchase. Her next aspect, a square to Mars, tells us there would be some disagreement involving price because Mars rules the merchant's money. However, her final aspect was a parallel to Jupiter, ruling both the merchant and the end-of-the-matter fourth house. So after a bit of "negotiating," the client was able to purchase the ring at a fair price. The final parallel to Jupiter, posited in the election twelfth house, was also an indication of temporary help behind the scenes. This came in the form of the appraiser, who helped my client determine a fair price. The Moon was decreasing in light and favored the buyer by bringing the price down. In this instance, the mutable angles were also to the buyer's advantage. They assisted in creating a flexible environment in which the parties were able to finally reach a compromise.

Election to Purchase a Car

Once again, the second house is a primary consideration when making any purchase. Its natural ruler, Venus, should be strong in any election to purchase something. It should also be well aligned with the Ascendant, the Ascendant ruler, or the Moon. Automobiles are ruled by Mercury

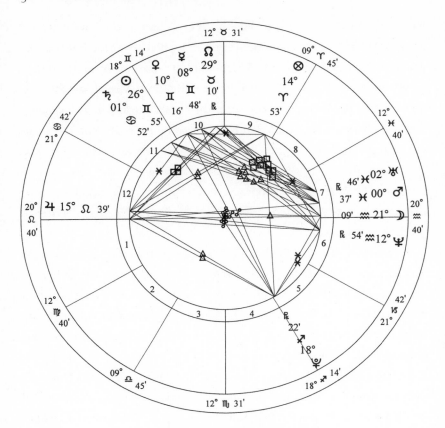

Purchase Car Election Chart
June 18, 2003 / 9:50 AM EDT / Flushing, New York
Placidus Houses

and fall into the third house. The planet Mars is considered because it rules machinery. When purchasing a new car that is being made to your specifications, the purchase takes place when you sign the contract. A contract is binding and costly if broken. Therefore, I consider the signing of the contract as the moment of finality. However, if purchasing a used car from a private person, the purchase takes place when the money changes hands. The same applies to a car purchased from a used-car dealer.

Mercury, Mars, and Venus should be direct for the purchase of an automobile, and well aligned with the Moon and/or the planet ruling the first house. It is always helpful to strengthen Mercury when a contract is being executed. Try to select a day when the Moon is decreasing in light, as this helps to lower the price of any purchase. The Moon in a fixed sign is helpful if you plan to keep the car for a long time.

Here is an example of an undemanding election date because the client had already made up his mind about the car he wanted. His purpose, with this election, was to make sure there would be no trouble with his new car, and that the process would be problem-free. The client is represented by the Sun in Gemini, the sign of automobiles, and the Moon, which in this instance is also a co-ruler of the seller because it is situated in the seventh house. The Moon is applying to only one major aspect, a trine to the Sun. This is a good indication that the buyer and seller will reach an immediate agreement. Because the Moon has little activity for the remainder of the day, we can conclude that it may be a rather slow day for the dealership, and they are happy to make the sale. Both Mars and Uranus, which co-rule the seventh house, are in an out-of-sign trine to the Sun, confirming this assumption.

The dealer's money is shown by the eighth house, ruled by retrograde Neptune. We can conclude that his resources are somewhat lacking, which should favor the buyer. My client's money is shown by the second-house ruler, Mercury in Gemini, the natural ruler of automobiles. It is applying to conjunct Venus, ruling the election third house, confirmation of the desired purchase. Both Mercury, the natural ruler of cars, and Venus, ruling the election third house, are accidentally dignified in an angular house. Further, Mercury is dignified in its own sign, giving us validation that the car will be sound and an excellent purchase. Both planets are sextile to Jupiter, so we can describe the automobile as luxurious and likely to last a long time. Fixed signs on the angles and the Moon in fixed Aquarius attest to that. The sign Aquarius is a good choice because it also rules mechanical things and transport vehicles. Fixed signs are always a plus for long-term results or if you want your purchase to last forever. The Moon is decreasing in light, which helped the client to negotiate a deal that was better than the sticker price.

THIRD-HOUSE ELECTIONS

Third-house elections include most Mercury-ruled matters such as the signing of papers, contracts, and agreements, taking a class, or passing a test. The third house also encompasses short trips, dealings with neighbors and siblings, and important announcements or speeches. In this age of media coverage, those in public office often seek an electional astrologer to select a date and time to make an important announcement.

Election to Pass an Examination

The third house and Mercury are the natural rulers of tests and examinations, whereas Jupiter and the ninth house rule licensing. Mercury should be strong by sign, favorably aspected, and direct in motion when selecting a date to schedule an examination. The only time a retrograde Mercury is acceptable is when you are repeating the test, and in that case the Moon should be in good alignment with Mercury. If applying for a license, consider Jupiter and the ninth house.

For any test, make certain to reinforce the third house of your election chart. You can do this by placing a benefic there in good aspect to the Ascendant or its ruler. Your objective is to link the first house with the third house by way of positive applying aspects. The Moon as a co-

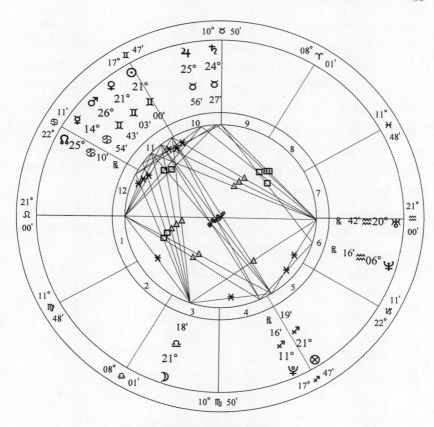

Examination Election Chart

June 11, 2000 / 10:25:37 AM CDT / Minneapolis, Minnesota

Placidus Houses

ruler of the first-house person can always be used to tie the action together. The tenth house is the house of success. If you are able to add it to the mix, all the better. Try to place Mercury in its sign of dignity or exaltation, as it adds strength to the matter. Mercury in the third house well aligned with the Moon, the Ascendant, or the Ascendant ruler is also beneficial. Keep the malefics out of the third house, because this can complicate matters. In the case of licensing, the same applies to the ninth house. Saturn brings delays, Uranus unexpected complications, and Pluto the possibility of loss.

The fourth house in any election chart will show the end result of the matter. When we look to the fourth house for confirmation of a successful outcome, we are looking for positive aspects between the rulers of the fourth house and the rulers of the first house or of the electional matter itself. Any planet in a house is a co-ruler of that house and may also be considered. In any election, reinforce the house pertaining to the matter. The Moon should be favorable to that house and/or its ruler. When taking a test, the electional time should correspond with the moment you pick up the pen and begin your test. However, if you are taking a correspondence course at home and sending in a final exam, the significant time is when the test is mailed.

The client requested an election date to pass an examination, the result of which would be certification to practice her chosen vocation. Here is another example of a fairly uncomplicated election. In this instance, the test would be taken at home and then mailed to the examiner. Therefore, the crucial time is when the completed test is dropped into the mailbox. Tests and examinations are third-house matters, and licensing falls into the ninth house. The Sun, ruling the client, is appropriately placed in Gemini, the natural ruler of tests and examinations. It is strengthened by conjunction to Venus and Mars, and is applying to both planets. Venus rules the election tenth house of success, and Mars the ninth house of licensing.

On this day, the Moon, always a co-ruler of the person initiating, was in Libra, so we placed it in the election third house applying to trine all the Gemini planets. The Moon applying to the planets ruling the client, the test, and the houses of success and licensing is a pretty good indication that she will pass the test and attain certification. The Moon's final aspect, a trine to Mars, ruling the election ninth house of licensing, is confirmation of this. Further, Mars is co-ruler of the end-of-the-matter fourth house, giving added corroboration.

Mercury, the natural ruler of examinations, is in Cancer and disposed by the Moon, whose aspects are only favorable. The Moon had just passed a trine to Uranus in the sixth house of work. This is of interest because the test was to pass an astrology exam. Uranus rules astrology, is in the sixth house of work, and is part of a grand trine involving the Sun, Venus, Mars, and the Moon. This configuration attests to the talent of the individual and also to the strong likelihood of her success as an astrological consultant. This is a perfect example of the universe responding to the need at hand. The client's intended goal was a foregone conclusion, and I had very little to do with it.

Election to Travel by Car

Another third-house matter is an automobile trip. The significant time is when you get in your car and commence the trip. Mercury and Mars rule automobiles and machinery. They should be well aligned to Venus and/or Jupiter if it is a pleasure trip, and to the Sun and/or Saturn if a business trip. If the trip is for recreational purposes, the Moon in Leo or one of the travel signs (Gemini and Sagittarius) is beneficial. Of course, we want easy aspects between the Moon or first-house ruler and the planet ruling the election third house. If the trip is a lengthy one, the ruler of the ninth house should also be considered. A benefic in the third house is always helpful, or place a benefic on the Ascendant, or in the fifth or ninth house trine the Ascendant. To ensure safety, avoid any difficult aspects

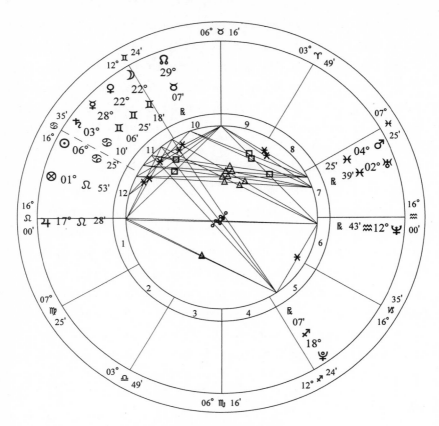

Automobile Trip Election Chart
June 28, 2003 / 8:46:04 AM EDT / Valhalla, New York
Placidus Houses

between Mars, Mercury, and Uranus. Also, the Ascendant ruler and the Moon should not be in any difficult aspect with Uranus.

The client, who avoids travel by air whenever possible, wanted to drive from upstate New York to Florida and back. This was to be a vacation trip with friends and family, and they were all traveling together in a rather large van. The significant time is when they all get into the van and drive off. Jupiter on the Ascendant describes both the distance to be driven and the cheerful nature of this adventure. We have the added benefit of the protective influence of Jupiter conveyed to everyone, since this was a group effort. Jupiter is disposed by the Sun, ruling the client and posited in the eleventh house of friendships and social acquaintances. Jupiter also rules the fifth house of fun, and this was a vacation trip.

The Moon, co-ruler of the client, is applying to conjunct Venus, ruling the election third house of the car trip. Venus also rules the tenth house of success. The Moon making few aspects indicates that the drive itself will be relatively uneventful. Her last aspect is a conjunction to Mercury, the natural ruler of car trips. Mercury is dignified in its own sign, and indicates that the vehicle will get them there safely. We see further evidence of a safe trip with Venus, ruling the election third house, in conjunction with the other planets. We look to the end-of-the-matter fourth house for added confirmation. It is co-ruled by Mars in conjunction with Uranus. The conjunction of Mars and Uranus is a favorable one because it is well aligned with the Sun and Saturn and not receiving any difficult aspects. Both planets are also in an out-of-sign trine with Mercury. We can conclude that this vacation trip will be packed with more than a few exciting surprises. The ninth house of distance is also ruled by Mars in Pisces, and describes the oceanfront rental where they were headed. Since this was to be a rather long trip, we wanted to keep any difficult planets out of the first quadrant. This election accomplished what we set out to do.

FOURTH-HOUSE ELECTIONS

The fourth house is the main consideration when moving into a new home, or when buying or selling a home. It would also be considered for the purchase or sale of a building, land, or any real estate. Together with the third house, it is considered when signing a lease or renting property for personal use. Any purchase or sale would require an agreement between two parties. Therefore, the first and seventh houses are considered together with the fourth house, representing the property or home. Buying and selling anything would include an analysis of the second and eighth houses of money to be exchanged.

Election to Buy or Sell a Home

Buying and selling falls under the domain of the second house, and to a lesser extent the eighth house. Therefore, the natural rulers of these houses, Venus and Mars, should be strong and direct in motion at the time of any purchase or sale. Mercury, planet of agreements and legal documents, should also be unafflicted and direct in motion. Mercury and Venus in good alignment is always beneficial.

In any purchase, the Ascendant and its ruler represent the buyer, while the Descendant and its ruler describe the seller. If you are the seller, it is the other way around. It is important to have good aspects between these two rulers to achieve an agreement. Try to keep the challenging planets away from the angles and particularly out of the first, fourth, and seventh houses.

The property for purchase or sale is shown by the Moon, the natural ruler of the fourth house, and any planet in the fourth house. Therefore, the Moon and the rulers of the first, seventh, and fourth houses must be in good aspect to each other to achieve the desired outcome. In this case, the Moon plays a dual role because she is the natural ruler of homes and real estate, and co-ruler of the first-house person, so keep her strong and favorable to the other rulers of the matter.

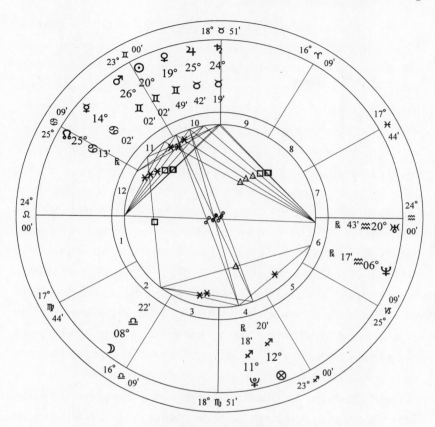

Purchase Home Election Chart
June 10, 2000 / 11:18:40 AM EDT / Asheville, North Carolina
Placidus Houses

Any planet in the fourth house will also describe the property. If Neptune is there, it warns of water damage, leaks, or flooding. It may also indicate beachfront property. The tenth house indicates the current value of the home or real estate. Any planet posited there will describe its worth. The second house represents the money of the person for whom you are doing the election. Try to strengthen this house, and make sure its ruler is in good alignment with the other significators.

Remember to keep in mind the person for whom you are preparing the election. If you represent the seller, then the Ascendant and its ruler indicate the seller, and the Descendant and its ruler represent the probable buyer. Always try to strengthen the first house and/or its ruler. Avoid difficult aspects to the ruler of the fourth house and especially to the Moon. The same applies to the rulers of the first and seventh houses. Ideally, place the rulers of the first, fourth, and seventh houses and the Moon in good alignment with each other. Try to avoid difficult aspects with Mars, Saturn, Uranus, Neptune, and Pluto. Always try to make use of a benefic planet, and if possible place it in the house representing your client, or in the house of the electional matter.

Try to keep the difficult planets away from the angles and particularly out of the first, second, fourth, and seventh houses. Fixed angles are considered beneficial for the purchase of property one hopes to keep for a long time. However, for a quick sale, cardinal angles are best. For any purchase or sale, it is always best to avoid retrograde Mercury, Venus, and Mars. Most important is a strong Moon, free from difficult aspects. The Moon in the sign of Taurus or Cancer is particularly favorable for the purchase of real estate.

An election to buy or sell property or a home should correspond with the time you sign the contract and hand it over to the broker, the attorney, or whoever is acting as agent. If done by mail, use the time you drop the signed contract into the mailbox. There is a secondary consideration, and that is the time you list your property for sale with the broker. Or, if acting as your own agent, the time you place an ad or "for sale" sign on the lawn. When purchasing, consider the time you make a verbal offer to the owner or their agent. You may want to set up election charts for each of these events to ensure the outcome you desire.

This election was done for a couple who wanted to purchase a landmark property for restoration. The home was a lovely old Victorian in need of extensive repair, but they were anxious to take it on. The objective is to reach an agreement. Therefore, we consider the first and seventh houses. The client is the prospective buyer, so Leo, the Sun, and the Moon represent the couple, and Aquarius, Uranus, and Saturn, the sellers. The Sun in Gemini is elevated and applying to trine retrograde Uranus. Uranus by retrograde motion is also applying to the Sun. Two planets mutually applying to each other indicate mutual agreement. Further, since the aspect is almost exact and Uranus operates quickly, the two parties would reach a prompt agreement.

The election fourth house, its rulers, Mars and Pluto, and the Moon describe the home and property. Retrograde Pluto in the fourth house rightly described this property as run down and in need of extensive repair. It will require major reconstruction, but the result should be favorable. This is indicated by the Moon applying to only positive aspects, including a trine to Venus, which rules the election tenth house. The tenth house shows the current value of the real estate. The Sun, Venus, and Jupiter in the election tenth house describe property that is quite valuable and priced accordingly. However, Saturn also situated there depreciates the value somewhat. Indeed, the property had been neglected for some time. This should enable the buyers to negotiate a slightly better price. Another indication that the home will appreciate in value is the fact that Pluto is disposed by Jupiter in the tenth house, suggesting that once the renovation is undertaken, value will be restored. The Moon in the second house of the client's money is applying to the Sun. She connects the home with the buyer, and her final aspect is a trine to Mars. Mars co-ruling the end-of-the-matter fourth house confirms the result we want.

Election to Move into a New Home

Moving into a new residence is considered a fourth-house matter. In my part of the country, requesting a date to move is commonplace since people tend to relocate frequently. Moving into a new home applies to wherever you call home, whether it is an apartment, house, or trailer. The most important consideration is the Moon. She is always a co-ruler of the first-house person, and in this instance also represents the home. We want easy aspects between the Ascendant ruler and the planet ruling the fourth house of the election. If you plan to stay put, a fixed Moon or fixed angles are beneficial, and avoid placing Uranus in an angular house. The time of the election should correspond with the moment you open the door and move the first item into the new residence.

This is a very simple election because we are working with only the first and fourth houses. The Moon is the natural ruler of home and family, so we selected a day when the Moon was making only positive aspects. The Moon rules the client and is strong in her natural house. Her first applying aspect is a sextile to Pluto in the work-related sixth house. This is interesting because the move was the result of a job change for the client. She next applies to trine Venus, ruling the home itself. This was a new home, and Venus in Aquarius perfectly described the home. It was of modern architecture with all sorts of high-tech installations throughout.

The Moon's final aspect is a trine to Saturn, ruling the election seventh house and co-ruling the eighth. This is a pretty good sign that the client and his spouse would benefit financially from this move. The Moon's final aspect to Saturn adds permanence to the move as well. They had requested a date that would support their intentions of remaining in this place for a long time. The fourth house, showing the end of the matter, confirms a positive outcome. The Moon is trine its ruler. Finally, all the more troublesome planets are posited in succedent or cadent houses, including Uranus, planet of sudden changes.

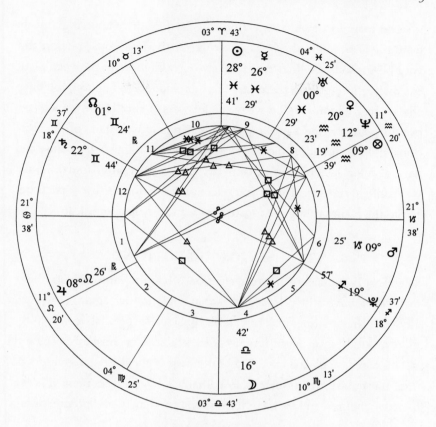

Moving In Election Chart
March 19, 2003 / 12:22 PM EST / Brooklyn, New York
Placidus Houses

The main focus in any election is to have positive applying aspects from the Moon. She is always a co-ruler of the first-house person and your best resource. Whenever you have easy alignments between planets, make those planets the rulers of your election. Whenever you have challenging alignments between planets, make sure those planets are not the primary rulers of your election. The natural rulers of the electional matter should be direct in motion and unafflicted. Try to use the natural rulers whenever you can. The end-of-the-matter fourth house will confirm the outcome of your election. Look for positive aspects between the planet ruling the fourth house and any key significator.

FIFTH-HOUSE ELECTIONS

The most requested fifth-house election is one for gambling, so I have included some of the primary rules that apply in this regard. However, anything that assumes risk or can be considered speculative would require an analysis of the fifth house. One's talents, creative interests, and hobbies are also placed here. The fifth house is considered in matters of love, unbounded relationships, love affairs, and entertainment. It is the focus of children and their circumstances, pregnancy, and procreation.

Election for Gambling I

Entire books have been written about the right time to win at games of chance. Here we will discuss some of the necessary principles to assist you in achieving a positive outcome. However, this is not meant to be a comprehensive discussion of the subject. As mentioned earlier, electional astrology is much more effective when the natal chart shows evidence of success in the matter. This is above all true when it comes to luck. Winning is substantiated in the birth chart. In addition, when attempting to win, it is essential that the natal chart be activated by positive transits. It is not unusual to see three or more transits to the natal chart at the time of a win. These usually involve the second and eighth houses of money, the fifth house of gambling, the tenth house of success, and the eleventh house of surprise. The natal Ascendant and Sun are also involved.

All games of chance, lotteries, contests, betting, and speculation come under the rulership of the fifth house. It might be a good day for winning if the natal ruler of your fifth house were activated by transit. In particular, the Sun, Venus, or Jupiter making an aspect to the fifth house or its ruler would signal the possibility of success. The fifth house of your birth chart is almost always active and may include (1) planets transiting through the fifth house; (2) a planet conjunct the fifth-house cusp; (3) a planet transiting through the fifth house and trine the Ascendant; (4) a planet transiting through the fifth house and at the same time making an aspect to the ruler of the fifth house—this is a strong day to win.

Lunations are often involved in setting the tone for a possible win. When a new Moon, full Moon, or eclipse activates one of the money houses, or the fifth or eleventh house, this can be an indication of changes in finances. Consider the other transits to evaluate the probability of winning. Uranus is usually involved with a major win. Watch for Uranus to make an aspect to your fifth-house cusp, its ruler, or a planet in the fifth house. This may be an indication of sudden good fortune. If Uranus is transiting through the fifth house, watch for it to make an aspect to the ruler of the fifth house. That may be a particularly good day if other factors are in play.

Once you have concluded that the natal chart is active, an election chart to win something must strengthen the fifth house. The Sun, the natural ruler of chance, should be strong by sign and in good alignment with the Ascendant and the Moon in the election chart. Try placing the Sun in the fifth house in trine to the Ascendant. Since the Moon is a co-ruler of the person initiating, she should apply to the ruler of the fifth house or a planet therein. You can enhance the election fifth house by placing Venus, the Sun, Jupiter, or the Moon there in trine to the Ascendant. It is also beneficial to place the ruler of your natal Ascendant in the election fifth house in trine to the Ascendant. The Part of Fortune is often evident in charts for a major win. In an election chart, place it in the fifth house trine the Ascendant or conjunct the cusp. The Part of Fortune conjunct the election Ascendant, the second-house cusp, or the eighth-house cusp is very helpful as well.

The second and eighth houses are always involved in winning money or prizes because these are the money houses. They are naturally in square aspect to the fifth house of speculation. The eleventh house of hopes, wishes, and surprise is also involved with winning, and it forms a natural opposition to the fifth house of speculation. This may be the reason that the so-called hard aspects seem to work best for winning. When planets are situated in any of these houses, they are in hard aspect to the fifth-house planets, and provide the tension associated with sudden wins. This is one time when the hard aspects seem to work best, but only when they are supported by the softer contacts. Experience has shown that the hard aspects activate, while the softer ones impart luck and ease of accomplishment. In an election to win, keep Saturn out of the second, fifth, eighth, and eleventh houses. These are the houses associated with winning, and Saturn in any one will lessen the win.

If you have ever won anything, try setting up an event chart with the date, time, and place of the win. You will notice that the cusps of your event chart were making contact with your natal chart. Of course, an exact birth time is necessary to do this kind of research. However, if you are inclined to keep records of your wins, you will find that there is contact between the two charts when you win. In an election chart for gambling, we are attempting to recreate what occurs naturally. The planets that rule your money houses and the fifth and eleventh houses are considered your gambling planets. These are normally active at the time of a win.

An election for gambling should always be set up for the place where you plan to play. The time should correspond with the moment you throw the dice, pull the lever, or place your first bet. This area of as-

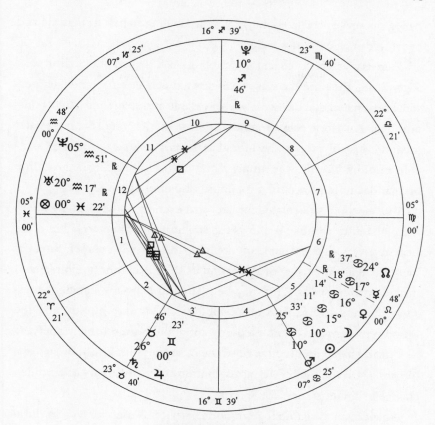

Gambling Election Chart I
July 1, 2000 / 11:08:32 PM EDT / Uncasville, Connecticut
Placidus Houses

trology is very specialized, but if you are willing to invest the time and effort, it can be quite rewarding.

Here is an election chart for gambling. As it turned out, Sharon won a car during the time she was playing on a dollar slot machine. Her personal transits on that day were very favorable and suggested a lucky outing. The new Moon eclipse earlier the same day activated Sharon's natal second house of money and hinted at the possibility of winning a sizeable amount. Then it was simply a matter of looking for the best time on that day to reinforce the fifth house of gambling.

The election is calculated for later that evening at the location where she planned to gamble. It allows the stellium of planets to fall into the fifth house, with the Ascendant applying to trine each planet. Interestingly, the Ascendant sign of Pisces and its ruler, Neptune, are often connected with big wins. This may be related to Neptune's ability to dissolve barriers and expand all possibilities. Neptune, Jupiter, and the Moon represent the client. Neptune and Jupiter are mutually applying to a trine aspect, and Jupiter rules the election tenth house of success. Neptune is in the sign of Aquarius, hinting at the possibility of a sudden change in circumstances for Sharon.

An election for gambling is unique in that it is used for a short duration, and is meant to set things in motion. We therefore use the house cusps to activate the planets. The Ascendant moves faster than any planet, at the rate of one degree every four minutes. Here it will apply to trine each fifth-house planet over a period of approximately one-and-three-quarters hours. The Ascendant's first aspect is a trine to Mars, ruling the election second house of money. Almost simultaneously it squares Pluto, confirmation of the hard and soft aspects working together to produce wins. Pluto is the natural ruler of the eighth house of other people's money and rules the election ninth house of luck. Sharon began winning almost immediately, and her streak continued for most of the time she was playing until she won the car. The fifth-house Moon first applies to a conjunction with Venus, the natural ruler of money and the ruler of the election eighth house of money from others. She then conjuncts Mercury, ruling the end of the matter. Her final aspect is a sextile to Saturn in the automobile third house. Saturn also describes the planning that went into this project. We had been working toward this end for quite some time.

As mentioned earlier, experience has shown that the more challenging alignments are always present during times of substantial wins. This was first evident in Sharon's birth chart. The solar eclipse that day activated her second house of money. Together with Mars and Venus, it was in square aspect to her natal Sun in Aries. These transits activated a T-square involving Sharon's second, fifth, and eleventh houses. The client has what is termed a gambling chart. On such occasions, the election chart can be used to pinpoint the best time to win.

Election for Gambling II

This chart was done for a Sagittarius friend who likes to gamble. I had been working with her for several months and was familiar with her birth chart. On this particular day, transiting Venus would conjunct her natal Ascendant. She had transiting Pluto and Mars traveling through her natal fifth house, and this election served to activate her natal chart.

The client is shown by the Sun in Libra and the Moon in Aries. The Moon is in the ninth house of luck and is applying to trine Mars, ruling the ninth house. This is a good sign that luck plays a role in the matter. Jupiter conjunct the tenth house of success is further evidence of good luck in view of the fact that it rules the fifth house of gambling. The Sun, ruling the client, is trine to Neptune, the planet often associated with winning. Neptune rules the election eighth house of money from others, and is further evidence of the possibility of winning on this day. Neptune in the sign of Aquarius supports this conclusion. Pluto, the natural ruler of the eighth house of other people's money, conjunct the election fifth house of gambling gives added support. The Moon will next oppose Mercury, ruler of the second house. This warns that the

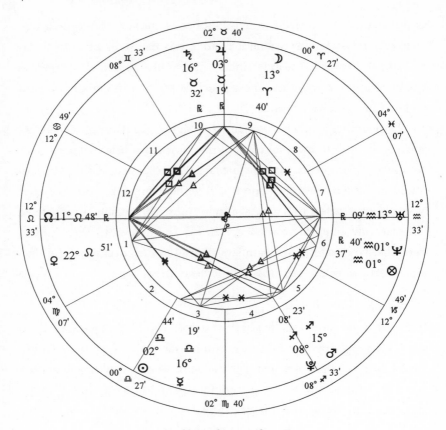

Gambling Election Chart II
September 26, 1999 / 2:41 AM EDT / Atlantic City, New Jersey
Placidus Houses

client will likely invest a considerable amount to accomplish her goal. Her final trine to Venus, however, indicates that the outcome will be favorable. Venus rules the tenth of success and is the natural ruler of money.

Uranus is almost always involved with substantial wins because it is the planet of unexpected surprises. Anyone who has gambled in a casino knows there is a certain electricity in the air, and Uranus conjunct the seventh house aptly describes the excitement surrounding this event. Uranus was trine to Mercury, ruling the election second house of her money, and as the Ascendant/Descendant cusps moved forward to activate that trine, she won $4,800 on a dollar slot machine. Since the Moon in Aries was applying to form a grand trine with Mars in the election fifth house and Venus in the first, she was able to continue for about an hour, and eventually walked away with over $7,200. By the time the Ascendant moved into Virgo, the streak was over.

In order to achieve this kind of result, the natal chart must indicate the potential for winning. My friend has a gambling chart. She was born with her Sagittarius Sun and Mars in the fifth house of gambling. She also has Neptune in the natal second house squaring those placements. This is an ideal setup for winning because whenever those planets are activated by transit, the opportunity resurfaces. The hard aspects in her natal chart connect with the houses of money and gambling. However, she also has a grand trine connected with her fifth house, which supports success in gambling. It is important to have evidence of the potential to win in the natal chart. Otherwise, the potential for loss is magnified.

SIXTH-HOUSE ELECTIONS

The sixth house is considered in all matters pertaining to one's routine work activities and voluntary labor. When opening an office to do one's work, consider this house. If making a change in employment, consider this house together with the tenth. It is also important for the acquisition and care of a pet. When choosing a health care professional or schedul-ing a routine physical, enhance the sixth house along with the first house.

Election to Acquire a Pet

The significant time is when the necessary papers are signed to transfer ownership and pedigree. If paperwork is not involved, then use the time when the money changes hands. If adopting a pet, the time you take possession is the moment of finality.

Mercury is most important in these matters because it rules both small animals and the signing of papers. Therefore, Mercury should be direct and strong in the election chart. Try to place Mercury in good alignment with the Ascendant ruler and the Moon. By way of derivative houses, the eleventh house shows the pet's health. Therefore, easy as-pects between the planets ruling the sixth and eleventh houses is a plus. This will ensure that the pet is healthy and is likely to live a long and happy life. Try to strengthen the sixth house of pets. You may accom-plish this by placing the Sun, Venus, or Jupiter there, or place Mercury in the sixth house in good alignment with the Moon. Any agreement between two parties should include favorable aspects between the rulers of the first and seventh houses.

The client, a professional dog breeder, will sometimes purchase a pedigree animal to complement her line. On this occasion, she asked me to select a good day to purchase a new puppy. This is an example of an election to address two needs: the desire to add to her business re-sources, and to acquire a healthy, productive puppy. We should there-fore consider the sixth house and its natural ruler, Mercury, along with the tenth house and its natural ruler, Saturn.

The client is shown by the Moon, well placed in its natural fourth house. The Moon is applying to trine Mercury, planet of small animals. Mercury is exalted by sign, an indication that the puppy will prove to be an exceptional animal. Although it is in the seventh house, it is conjunct

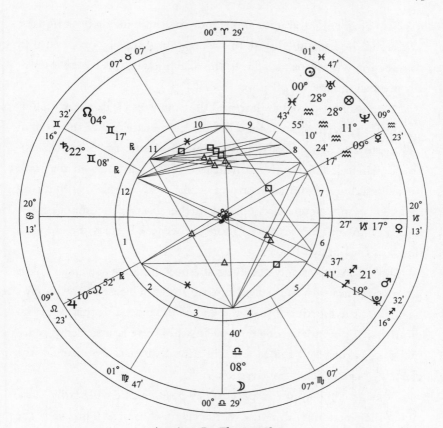

Acquire a Pet Election Chart
February 19, 2003 / 2:00 PM EST / Catskill, New York
Placidus Houses

the cusp of the eighth house and is therefore influencing both houses. The eighth house is the house of procreation. Mercury on its cusp in conjunction with Neptune adds to the likelihood of this puppy eventually producing superior offspring.

The sixth house further describes the puppy and is ruled by Jupiter. Jupiter is in the election second house, an indication that this animal will add to the resources of the client. Jupiter in trine aspect to the sixth-house planets confirms this conclusion. Pluto and Mars in the sixth house describe the animal as strong, fertile, and capable of producing many offspring. Venus also posited in the sixth house supports the health of the animal, and even more so because it rules the eleventh house of the puppy's health.

The Moon makes only one difficult aspect, a square to Venus. This is interesting because Venus rules both the eleventh house of the puppy's health and the fourth house of the end of the matter. Is this aspect indicative of a potential problem? The answer is no because Venus is disposed by Saturn and the Moon will trine Saturn. It does reflect the client's worry, which is unwarranted.

Otherwise, the Moon's aspects are all positive. She will sextile Mars, ruling the election tenth house of the client's business. This offers the opportunity to add to her business. The Moon will trine Saturn, the natural ruler of business, confirming that this purchase would be a good business decision. Saturn rules the election seventh house, indicating that the two parties can reach an agreement. The Moon will finally trine Uranus in the reproduction eighth house, another strong indication that the outcome will be as expected.

Election for a Physical Examination

Although this is a routine matter, many people are uneasy about going to the doctor, so I am often asked to pick a date and time that will ensure a problem-free outcome. While it is not possible to say that a person will get a clean bill of health, it is possible to create a favorable envi-

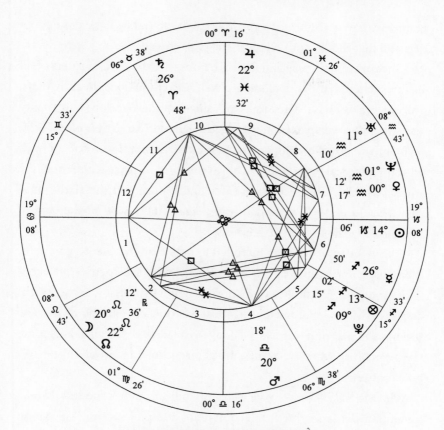

Physical Examination Election Chart
January 4, 1999 / 5:00 PM EST / Flushing, New York
Placidus Houses

ronment. The objective is to ensure that all the tests will be done properly and that the doctor will serve the patient well.

Once again, Mercury and the sixth house are the natural rulers of all health-related matters, including physical examinations, healthy diets, and physical exercise. The Sun is indicative of one's stamina and vitality and should be well placed in the election chart. The sixth house should be free from any difficult planets. The election first house corresponds with the physical body, and it is always helpful to place a benefic there when possible. The Ascendant ruler, the Moon, and the sixth-house ruler should be well aligned. Avoid placing the Moon in the sign of Scorpio or in the first or sixth house.

This is a simple election intended to help ease the client's concerns. It begins with the time of the appointment with the doctor. The client undergoing the physical examination is shown by Cancer on the Ascendant. The Moon in Leo helps set a positive tone and allay her fears. The Moon in a fixed sign imparts a feeling of steadiness. Cardinal angles are the best choice when we want a quick resolution, and in this instance a good option.

The Moon will first sextile Mars, an indication that she should take the initiative. Mars rules the election tenth house of success. The Moon then applies to a grand trine with Saturn and Mercury. Saturn rules the election seventh house of all others who may assist in the matter, and also co-rules the eighth house of their resources. This is a pretty good indication that those who may assist her will do so to the best of their ability. Furthermore, Saturn is well placed in its own natural house, confirming the professionalism of the health care workers.

The physical examination, the doctor's office, and the doctor are all shown in the sixth house of the election chart. The natural rulers of health, the Sun and Mercury, are well situated in that house. The Sun is applying to sextile Jupiter, ruling the doctor and the examination itself. The Ascendant will also trine Jupiter, so we can say the patient will feel comfortable with the doctor, and the overall experience will be a positive one. The Moon's last aspect is a trine to Mercury, the natural ruler of the sixth house of health. Mercury rules the election third house of tests. We can conclude that the examination, and the tests performed, will be unproblematic. The end of the matter is shown by Venus, dignified in its natural house. Her conjunction with Neptune says that in the end, all concerns will fade away.

SEVENTH-HOUSE ELECTIONS

The most requested election by far is that of a date and time to marry. Although the seventh house pertains to partnerships of all sorts, including business alliances, marriage is the primary subject associated with this house. The seventh house is also considered when beginning a lawsuit, forming a partnership, reaching an agreement with anyone, or when interacting with the public..

Election for Marriage I

A marriage election begins when the couple is pronounced man and wife. The marriage itself is shown by the seventh house. The groom is shown by the planet ruling the first house, and the bride by the planet ruling the seventh house. The natural rulers of marriage are Venus and Mars, so they are always co-significators of the marriage. Therefore, Venus and Mars should be in good alignment to each other and to the Moon. They should also be direct in motion. The election first- and seventh-house rulers should be in good aspect to each other and to the Moon. A positive aspect between Venus and Jupiter is very helpful in an election for marriage, or to form a business partnership.

A strong Moon is always important, and particularly so in an election for marriage because she rules women and children. The Moon should never be void-of-course. She should be in good aspect to the planets ruling the first and seventh houses, and/or to Venus and Mars, and free from any difficult aspects. Her final aspect must be a positive one, and a waxing Moon is desirable for a wedding date. *Since the Moon is a co-ruler of the person initiating action, she should always apply to a favorable aspect with the ruler of the house in question.* So the Moon should always apply to a favorable aspect with the ruler of the seventh house or a planet in the seventh house in a marriage election chart.

The Sun and Moon are the natural rulers of men and women, so a positive aspect between them is very beneficial. If possible, place the Sun and Moon above the horizon. This also applies to the benefics Venus and Jupiter. Planets in the upper half of the chart are elevated and prominent. Try to avoid any difficult aspects between the marriage rulers and Saturn, Uranus, Neptune, and Pluto. In particular, the Sun, Moon, and Venus should not apply to a difficult aspect with a malefic. Try to place Saturn, Uranus, Neptune, and Pluto in either a cadent or succedent house.

An election for marriage should enhance the seventh house. It is beneficial to place the ruler of the first house in the seventh house, and if possible, with the ruler of the seventh and/or Venus, the Sun, or Jupiter. The idea is to support the marriage itself and also the participants. Of course, the Moon should be favorable to the seventh house (in good alignment with the house cusp, or with a planet in the house, or with the ruler) and making only positive aspects to the marriage rulers. Concentrate primarily on a strong Sun, Moon, Venus, and Mars. Select fixed angles for stability and long-term commitment. Cardinal angles are the next best. The Moon should be strong by sign as well as unafflicted. She should make only positive applying aspects. Above all, she should not apply to a difficult aspect with Mars, Saturn, Uranus, Neptune, or Pluto.

When calculating the time for a marriage election, keep in mind that the marriage begins with the pronouncement of man and wife. Often you will be required to work within a specified time frame. This was the situation in selecting a marriage date for John and Susan. They had requested September or October of that year. While this election chart is not perfect, it is pretty good considering the time constraints. In

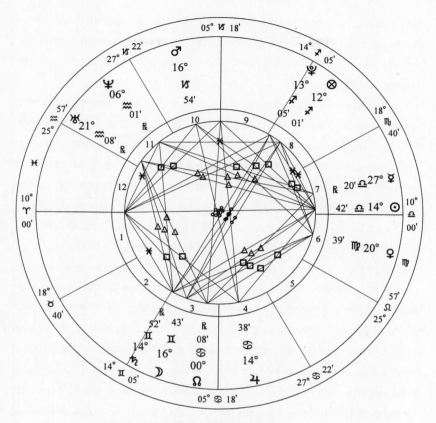

Marriage Election Chart I

October 7, 2001 / 6:12:31 PM EDT / Manhattan, New York

Placidus Houses

this instance, it was easy to use the trine between Mars and Venus by se-lecting a time of day that placed Libra on the cusp of the marriage house. The cardinal angles favor initiative and are suitable for a mar-riage election.

The primary consideration is always the house ruling the election matter, and here we have the Sun in the marriage house trine the Moon. The Sun and Moon in good alignment is always a plus, but especially for a marriage election because they are the natural rulers of men and women. When under certain time constraints, it is important to use whatever planets are well aligned. Then make those planets the rulers or the co-rulers of your election chart. Here Mars rules the groom. He is exalted by sign and house, and trine Venus, ruling the bride.

The Moon has a dual role. She co-rules the first-house person and is the natural ruler of women. Certainly, she is always an important con-sideration. In this election, she will apply to a square with Venus. At first glance this seems problematic. However, Venus is in mutual reception with Mercury, so the Moon can trine Venus. Further, Mars, ruling the first house, is also trine Venus, overcoming any difficulty. The Moon is otherwise unafflicted. She will next trine Uranus, and finally Mercury, which is in the election seventh house. The Moon also rules the end of the matter in this chart, and she is applying to a parallel with Jupiter in the fourth house. This gives confirmation of a successful outcome.

Notice that Mercury is retrograde in this election chart. However, it was a second marriage for both parties. Under the circumstances, retro-grade Mercury is acceptable because the bride and groom were repeat-ing their marriage vows. Mercury, though retrograde, is quite strong. It is accidentally dignified in the seventh house, and is in mutual reception with Venus. These two planets can change places, and each one is digni-fied in its natural house.

Election for Marriage II

The Moon is making only positive applying aspects in this election chart. Occasions when the Moon is completely free from any negative

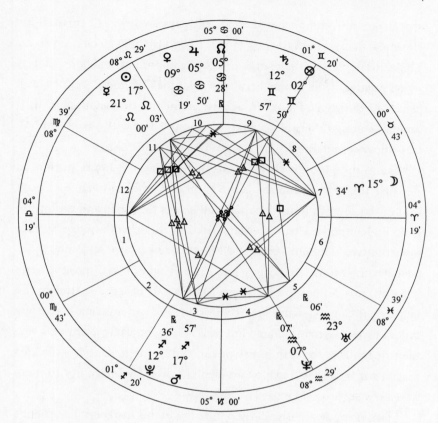

Marriage Election Chart II
August 9, 2001 / 10:05:16 AM EDT / New York, New York
Placidus Houses

aspects are few and far between. These days are always beneficial for electional matters because the Moon is so important in an election chart. The natural rulers of the matter are equally important, and here Venus is representative of the groom because it rules the first house. Venus is well placed in the sign of Cancer, and strengthened by conjunction with Jupiter. Among other things, Jupiter's conjunction with Venus symbolizes affluence, and the groom is a prominent businessman.

Again, the Moon is always a co-ruler of the first house person, in this case the groom, and she is the natural ruler of women. Her position in the seventh house of marriage brings the bride and groom together. Her applying trine to Mars, ruler of the seventh house, further joins the two. Though Venus and Mars are not in aspect, Venus is disposed by the Moon, connecting it to Mars by way of its dispositor. Mars in Sagittarius defines the marriage. Mars is part of a grand trine in fire linking the Sun, Mercury, and the Moon. We can anticipate a strong union, involving many shared interests. The Moon's final aspect, a sextile to Uranus in the fifth house of fun and children, supports the idea that this marriage will exhibit an element of spontaneity, not to mention a few surprises in regard to children.

Libra rising was particularly significant in this instance. The client's natal Sun is in Libra, and his Ascendant is in an early degree of Cancer. Therefore, the election served to support his natal chart—he benefited from transiting Venus and Jupiter conjunct his Ascendant. The election Sun is dignified in Leo. The luminaries in trine aspect is especially helpful in a marriage election because they represent the man and woman. The end-of-the-matter fourth house is ruled by Saturn, just separating from an opposition with Pluto. Separating aspects are indicative of what has already occurred. This is interesting because Pluto rules the second house of money. The groom financed the wedding, and this aspect accurately describes the substantial expenditure of money. Mars as a co-ruler of the second house, just separating from an opposition with Saturn, confirms this assumption.

Election for Marriage III

The couple requested a summer wedding, and we were fortunate to be able to take advantage of both Venus and the Moon in the marriage sign Libra. The groom is shown by Mars in the fifth house of the election chart, and by the Moon in the seventh house of marriage. Mars is considered strong when conjunct the Sun, and the Moon posited in the marriage house positively connects the bride and groom.

Once again, the Moon is making only positive aspects on this day. Her applying sextile to Mars further joins the two in the seventh house of marriage. The Moon's next aspect, a trine to Saturn, is quite fortunate. It gives stability and commitment to the relationship. Furthermore, Saturn, ruling the election tenth house of success, is a good omen for a long and lasting marriage.

The bride and the marriage itself are shown in the seventh house. Here, Venus, dignified in her own sign, together with the Moon in Libra, serve to strengthen the marriage house. Although Mars and Venus did not form a major aspect, the Moon is disposed by Venus, connecting it to Mars by way of its dispositor. The Moon is increasing in light and is virtually unafflicted. The Moon's condition is by far the most important consideration in the election chart. Her applying aspects bring the people together with the intended objective. Secondly, the house of the matter, and its rulers, should be free from difficult aspects. Though there are likely to be some planets in stressful alignment, as long as they are not connected with the house of the matter, your election will succeed. For confirmation, look to the Moon's final aspect and to the end-of-the-matter fourth house. Here, the Moon also rules the end of the matter, and her strong condition affirms a positive outcome.

The universe is always a perfect mirror of circumstances, thus the fifth house of children reflected this couple's strong desire to begin a family right away. Jupiter there is sure to increase the number, and eventually there may be three children. Three planets in the fifth house in the sign of children tend to support this conclusion. Time will tell.

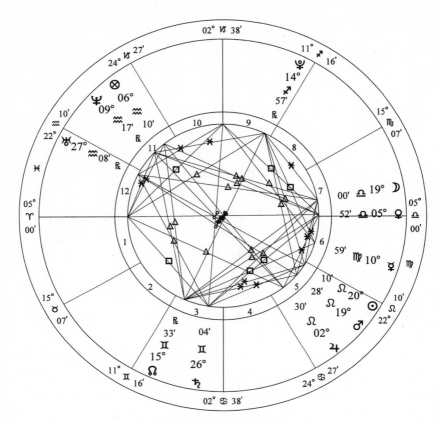

Marriage Election Chart III
August 12, 2002 / 9:42:07 PM EDT / Manhattan, New York
Placidus Houses

EIGHTH-HOUSE ELECTIONS

The eighth house is the primary focus when filing for bankruptcy, filing taxes, preparing a will, or setting up a trust. It is key when purchasing life insurance or managing joint finances. It represents the assets of the other person, and is therefore considered when reaching a financial settlement. It also represents the assets of one's spouse and is the house of alimony. The eighth house together with the first house is considered for surgery, and if a hospital stay is required, the twelfth house is part of the equation.

Election to File Tax Return

Once the tax return has been prepared, we send it off and hope to avoid a tax audit. This is a rather straightforward matter as the eighth house, Mars, and Pluto rule taxation and tax collectors, and the first house rules the person filing. The important time is when the tax return is dropped into the mailbox or at the post office.

Electional rulerships stem from horary astrology, which applies traditional planetary rulers. Therefore, Mars is considered the natural ruler of the eighth house. If you have an option, give precedence to the traditional ruler, with secondary consideration to the modern ruler. Try to keep the difficult planets out of the eighth and first houses, and out of the first quadrant. We want easy aspects between the first-house ruler, the Moon, and the planet ruling the election eighth house. We also want favorable alignments between the natural rulers of the first and eighth houses, Mars and Pluto, when possible. The Sun, Venus, or Jupiter in the eighth house in good aspect to the Ascendant or its ruler is protective. The Moon or the planet ruling the Ascendant posited in the twelfth house keeps a low profile.

This not-so-perfect election managed to accomplish the objective, which was to avoid a tax audit. This was a particular concern for the client because he had been audited in the past. The time constraints were limiting, and everything about this chart reflects the client's circumstances,

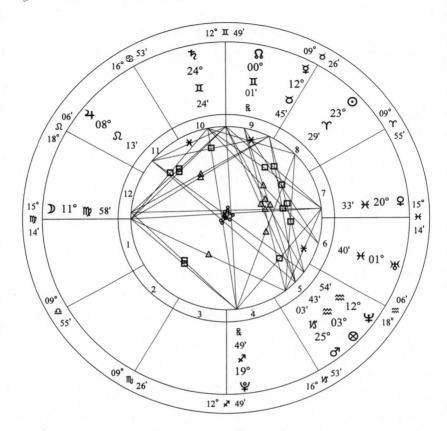

File Tax Return Election Chart
April 13, 2003 / 4:15 PM EDT / Manhattan, New York
Placidus Houses

including the hefty payment he was required to send to the IRS. However, the end result was satisfactory.

Mercury and the Moon represent the client, while Mars and the eighth house represent the tax authorities. The Moon first applies to a trine with Mercury, the natural ruler of papers. Mercury is in the ninth house of filing legal papers and in the money sign of Taurus. The Moon will next square Pluto, the natural co-ruler of taxes, and oppose Venus, the natural ruler of money. Venus rules the election second house of the client's money, and accurately describes the circumstances. The client was separated from a considerable sum of money he owed the tax authorities. Nevertheless, Venus is dignified by house, exalted by sign, and sextile to Mercury, ruling the client. So his money was sheltered, and an audit avoided.

The Moon's next aspect is a square to Saturn in the tenth house of authority. However, Saturn is disposed by Mercury, and the Moon will trine Mercury. We can conclude that should the client be challenged, he will prevail. The final aspect of the Moon is a trine to Mars, ruling the election eighth house. Mars is also the natural ruler of the eighth house, and in this chart is exalted in Capricorn. The Sun in the election eighth house is exalted in Aries. Together, they suggest that the client is protected from the worst. The Moon is placed in the veiled twelfth house. In this situation, it is an auspicious placement because it helps to keep the client out of sight. The end-of-the-matter fourth house contains retrograde Pluto, hinting at the probability that the IRS will forego examination.

Election to Settle an Insurance Claim

Here, the main focus is the eighth house of insurance companies. In most situations, when a claim is made, we would like to reach a settlement with the other party. Therefore, we also consider the seventh house of agreements, while the ninth house and Jupiter rule insurance adjustors. The second house is the client's money, and the eighth house

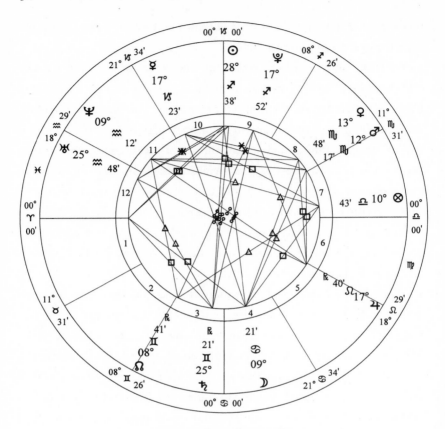

Insurance Claim Election Chart
December 20, 2002 / 11:58:51 AM EST / Flushing, New York
Placidus Houses

shows the assets of the insurers, so we want easy aspects between the rulers of these houses.

The first-house ruler and the Moon should be favorably aligned with the planets ruling the seventh and eighth houses. It is beneficial to have Mars and Venus in good alignment with each other, since they are the natural rulers of money and settlements. If possible, place a benefic in the second house and well aligned with the ruler of the eighth house, or let the Moon apply favorably to a planet in or ruling the eighth. The Moon in Libra, or Libra rising or on the seventh house cusp, favors a settlement.

The client had been trying to reach a settlement with her insurance company for several months, without success. They finally contacted her and said they were sending a second adjustor to her home on the date of the election chart. Since she had no choice in the matter, the best I could do was select the time. Fortunately, she was able to persuade them to arrive at the time we decided upon.

Since this is an adversarial environment, the seventh house represents the opponent. The client is characterized by Aries rising, and Mars is strong in the sign of Scorpio and in its natural eighth house. The Moon, co-ruler of the client, is strong in Cancer and applying to trine both Mars and Venus. This is a pretty good sign that she will prevail and be able to reach an agreement with them. Since this was to be a settlement on a homeowner's claim, the Moon in its natural fourth house is very helpful.

Notice that Mars and Venus rule the client, the opponent, and the assets of both parties. We wanted to strengthen the client's position and, if possible, weaken the opponent's. Venus in Scorpio is considered in detriment, and this weakness is reflected in the position of the opponent. It also describes the fragile finances of the client. However, Mars is stronger in that sign and favors my client's position. We see further confirmation of a successful outcome with Pluto co-ruling the eighth in the ninth house of the insurance adjustor. As the Ascendant moved forward to trine Pluto, and then Jupiter, ruler of the election ninth, we could expect a satisfactory offer. The settlement was reached, and the matter was dropped, as indicated by the Moon's final aspect, an opposition to Mercury. The insurance company also dropped the client, but not before the claim was satisfied. As always, the universe is a perfect mirror of the current circumstances.

NINTH-HOUSE ELECTIONS

The ninth house is considered when filing legal papers or when obtaining a license or certification. It is a primary consideration when entering college or any institution of higher learning. It is also the focus of air travel, and dealings with travel agents, publishers, attorneys, foreign people, and foreign countries. Extensive advertising to reach a broad audience, such as radio and television, is a ninth-house matter. Subjects relating to religion and faith are also ninth-house matters.

Election for Legal Proceedings

Although a lawsuit can be considered a seventh-house matter, the filing of papers for any legal proceeding is a ninth-house matter. An election for filing a lawsuit should feature a strong first house, as it represents the plaintiff or the person bringing the action. The seventh house and its ruler signify the defendant or opponent. The tenth house and its ruler show the judge or those passing judgment. The ninth house and its ruler represent the attorney for the first-house person. The fourth house and the Moon's final aspect indicate the end result or outcome of the matter. Mars, Venus, Saturn, and Jupiter are the natural rulers of the houses involved in legal proceedings. Jupiter rules attorneys and the filing of legal actions. Mercury, planet of agreements, contracts, and papers, is also considered.

To succeed in any legal action, reinforce the first house and its ruler, and place the first-house ruler in a stronger position than the ruler of the seventh house. Aries and Scorpio are particularly strong signs, as they seldom back down, and have the courage to see things through to the end. Mars in or ruling the ninth house in good aspect with the Ascendant or its ruler is quite favorable. It describes the attorney as assertive, and capable of representing the client's interests. The planet ruling the first house should be favorably aligned with the ninth- and tenth-house rulers. Otherwise, the Moon, always a co-ruler of the first-house person, should be in good alignment with these planets.

The relationship between the plaintiff and his attorney can be seen by the planets ruling those houses. If the ruler of the ninth house is in difficult aspect with the Ascendant ruler, the attorney may not work well for his client. To succeed in any legal action, the planets ruling the first, ninth, and tenth houses must be favorable to one another. Since not all lawsuits come to trial, an agreement can be reached when the first- and seventh-house rulers are in favorable alignment or in mutual reception. If the client is willing to settle out of court, then make certain those planets are in positive alignment. If a benefic is placed in the first house, the settlement will favor the plaintiff.

A lawsuit is initiated with the filing of the complaint. The attorney usually files the papers, so make certain he or she is willing to work with you. Of course, the main objective is always to strengthen the position of the client, and to make sure the ruling will go in the client's favor.

The plaintiff in this election is represented by Sagittarius rising. Jupiter, his ruling planet, is well placed in the ninth house, and trine to the Ascendant and all the first-house planets. Jupiter is further strengthened by mutual reception with the Sun. Since the ninth house represents the attorney and the actual filing of legal papers, this is a good indication that the case is a strong one in favor of the plaintiff. Jupiter also describes the attorney as an expert in his field, and the mutual reception indicates he is able to put himself in the client's shoes, so to speak.

The seventh house describes the defendant. Retrograde Saturn posited there weakens his position. Further, Mercury, ruling the seventh house, is

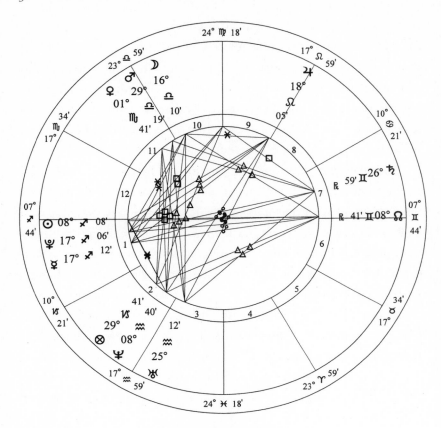

File Lawsuit Election Chart
November 30, 2002 / 7:40 AM EST / Cincinnati, Ohio
Placidus Houses

in the first house, suggesting that the defendant will more than likely yield to the plaintiff. This supposition is confirmed by an analysis of the tenth house. The tenth house describes the judge and is also ruled by Mercury. Both Mercury and the Moon favor the plaintiff. The Moon is always a co-ruler of the first-house person, and here she is in the tenth house of the one who will pass judgment. The Moon here can also describe the judge. In Libra, it suggests that he will be fair in his approach.

The Moon's favorable aspects to both the first-house rulers and the seventh-house rulers show that equal consideration will be given to both parties in this matter. However, the Moon is inclined to favor the plaintiff because of her status as co-ruler of that house. Mercury ruling the tenth house and posited in the first is confirmation that the ruling will go in favor of the plaintiff. We look to the end-of-the-matter fourth house for further corroboration. Neptune, the fourth-house ruler, is in the second house of the client's future, and is exactly sextile the Sun. This is confirmation enough. As it turned out, the lawsuit never went forward. It was settled, out of court, in favor of the plaintiff.

Election for Air Travel

Another ninth-house matter is travel by air. Our primary concerns are safety and, of course, a pleasurable experience. The natural rulers of air travel are Jupiter and the ninth house, ruling distance and foreign countries; Uranus, ruling airplanes and airports; and Mercury, ruling the air. However, Mercury rules all mechanical functions, so no matter what mode of transportation you choose, Mercury should be free from affliction. Mars is also considered because it rules the machinery itself. Local travel by automobile, bus, rail, or other ground vehicle is ruled by Mercury and the third house. Travel by water, cruising and boating, is ruled by the Moon and also Neptune.

When selecting a time for travel, it is beneficial to keep any difficult planets out of the first quadrant. Since most trips last for several hours, any difficult planet posited in either the first, second, or third house may reach the Ascendant, bringing its function along with it. The aspects to that planet would provide some indication of what to expect: Saturn may bring delays, Uranus, unexpected weather conditions, Neptune, unforeseen problems, and Pluto, hazardous conditions.

If you are planning a trip by air, reinforce the ninth house of your election chart. It is always beneficial to place a benefic planet in the ninth house trine the Ascendant. You can also place the Ascendant ruler in the ninth house trine the Moon. As always, the Moon should be free from affliction, and in this case, applying to a favorable aspect with the ruler of the ninth house. Uranus is the planet of unexpected complications, including accidents. If you are traveling by air, avoid difficult aspects to Uranus. A difficult aspect between Mars and Uranus is unfavorable for any kind of travel. Reinforce the Moon and the election ninth house and its ruler. If possible, place the Sun, Venus, or Jupiter in the ninth house trine the Ascendant.

Travel by automobile or other ground vehicle is ruled by Mercury. Your election third-house ruler should be favorable to Mercury and to the Moon. Try to avoid difficult aspects between Mercury, the Moon, the third-house ruler, and Uranus. Reinforce the third house by placing a benefic there in good aspect with the Ascendant or its ruler. If you are planning a cruise, take into account the relationship between the Moon and Neptune. These should be in good alignment with each other and with the Ascendant or its ruler. Reinforce the travel houses, the third house for short distance and the ninth house for long distance. If possible, place Jupiter, Venus, or the Sun in the third or ninth house and in good aspect to the Ascendant. As always, the Moon should be free from affliction and well aligned to the travel houses or their rulers.

Many people are uneasy about traveling by air, so this type of election is often requested by clients. The election time should correspond with the moment you leave your home, as this is the beginning of the trip. Therefore you needn't be concerned about the departure time of the flight.

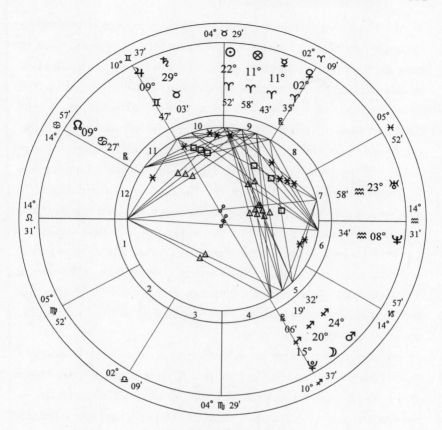

Air Travel Election Chart
April 12, 2001 / 1:40 PM EDT / Bayside, New York
Placidus Houses

This chart is an example of how to use an existing aspect and tie it to the important houses. On this day we had a trine between the Sun in Aries and the Moon in Sagittarius. It was easy to select a time when Leo would be on the Ascendant, thus representing the client. The Ascendant moves faster than any planet, and will move forward to trine the Sun in the ninth house of air travel. Venus, Mercury, the fortune node, and the Sun combine to strengthen the house of air travel. Mars, ruling that house, will also trine the Ascendant, confirming a positive experience.

The Moon, co-ruling the client, is in the fifth house of enjoyment. It is an appropriate placement because this was a vacation trip. She will first trine the Sun in the ninth house of distance. Her next aspect is a sextile to Uranus in the seventh house of others. The client traveled with two other girlfriends on this vacation. The Moon's final aspect, a conjunction to Mars, indicates that they will reach their destination without incident. Since Mars also co-rules the end-of-the-matter fourth house, it confirms a good outcome.

We always give added consideration to Uranus when selecting a time to travel by air. In this election chart, Uranus is sextile to the rulers of the event. Saturn had been in square aspect to Uranus for many months, but was now separating from that aspect. Therefore, it is not a concern, especially since neither planet is linked to the travel houses.

TENTH-HOUSE ELECTIONS

Another election commonly requested is that of a date and time to open a new business. The tenth house is the primary focus because it represents the business. It is also considered the house of success, and is given reinforcement when one's reputation or public image is the focus of an election. It shows one's profession, and is considered in an election to make a career change or begin a new occupation. It represents judges and those who hold power, and is therefore considered when an opinion is handed down or a judgment passed.

Election for Business I—Restaurant

The primary focus in a business election is the tenth house, its ruling planet, and any planet posited there. The Sun plays a major role in business charts, as do the natural rulers of business, Saturn and Jupiter. Therefore, try to have the Sun, Saturn, Jupiter, and the ruler of the tenth house strong and in good alignment.

Of course, the Moon should be applying by favorable aspect to the planets ruling the business. It is beneficial to place the natural ruler of the business matter in a strong position in the chart. For example, if opening a bookstore, the planet Mercury should be in high focus. You can place Mercury in the tenth house, or the sign Gemini on the tenth-house cusp. Mercury should also be direct in motion.

Venus is the natural ruler of money, and should therefore be strong in an election chart for business. She should be in good aspect to the other rulers and direct in motion. The eleventh house represents the money from the business. It is helpful to place Venus, Jupiter, or the Sun in the eleventh house to improve the cash flow of the business. Saturn and Jupiter, the natural rulers of business, should be well placed, in good aspect to each other, and direct in motion. Along with the Sun, they are important indicators of the success of any business. Make sure the Moon is well aligned with them. The Moon in Taurus is particularly good for business ventures.

As a way of supporting the business, place a benefic in the tenth house, or place the planet ruling the nature of the business there. You can place the business planets in good aspect with the Midheaven. The Moon should apply to a favorable aspect with at least one of the business rulers. It is essential to link the client with the business. If the ruling planets are not in aspect, you can always use the Moon. Try to look for days when the Sun, Saturn, and Jupiter are in good alignment, and then rotate the wheel so that the Midheaven receives favorable aspects from these planets.

Mars in the tenth house is considered very good for business. It is dignified by house, and reflective of the necessary drive to succeed. The Moon should always be strong and free from any difficult aspects involving the business rulers. Good aspects between the Sun, Moon, Saturn, and Jupiter will improve success in business. Although Saturn is a primary business significator, avoid placing Saturn in the tenth house as this can delay or curtail the growth of business. Instead, have Saturn sextile or trine the Midheaven or a planet in the tenth house. Neptune in the tenth house is also considered unfavorable for business, unless your business is related to music, art, or some other Neptunian endeavor.

The business election begins when the official signed papers are handed over to the registrar or clerk for filing. If submitting official papers by mail, the important time is when they are dropped into the mailbox. However, there is a secondary consideration and that is the "grand opening" of your business. In that case, the time you open your doors to the public is the moment of finality. If you are planning a party to mark the occasion, the same rule applies. You may choose to prepare an election for each event.

The primary consideration in a business election is the tenth house. It represents the business, and the eleventh house defines the income from the business. The Ascendant ruler should be linked with the business in some way. In the election chart for the restaurant, Mercury ruling both the Ascendant and the Midheaven shows that the client and his business are closely related. Furthermore, Mercury in Gemini is an accurate description of the dual role the client is undertaking. He is both the business owner and the head chef. This restaurant was the second one opened by the same owner.

This chart has many of the features we look for in a business election: a strong tenth house with the Sun conjunct the Midheaven, supported by Saturn on the ninth-house side for the long-term stability needed. Mars, planet of drive and ambition, is very positive in the tenth house, and the Moon applying to Jupiter and then Venus is strong in her

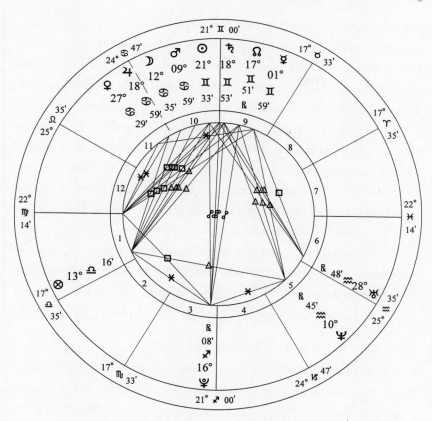

Business Election Chart I—Restaurant

June 12, 2002 / 12:53:23 PM EDT / Manhattan, New York

Placidus Houses

own sign. The Moon in Cancer is particularly favorable for the food business, and her conjunction to Jupiter is sure to increase the public appeal of this restaurant. The Moon in the tenth house also attracts public awareness and fame. We have the added benefit of a waxing Moon to assist in the growth of the business. The Moon's aspects are all favorable.

We were able to place Venus in the eleventh house of business income, and Jupiter is conjunct the cusp. Therefore, Jupiter adds benefit to both the tenth house of the business and the eleventh house of its assets. This is a pretty strong indication that the business will generate substantial income. Since Jupiter is co-ruler of the seventh house of the public, it tends to confirm this conclusion. The end-of-the-matter fourth house, also ruled by Jupiter, is confirmation of a favorable outcome, as is the Moon's final aspect. She will conjunct Venus in the eleventh house of business income. Venus ruling the election second house of the client's money adds corroboration of financial success.

Election for Business II—Photography Studio

This election was done for a photographer who traveled quite a bit in his line of work, and was seldom in one place. However, at the time he requested this election, he wanted to open a small gallery where he could exhibit his work when he was in town. This election represents the opening of his new studio, which would also serve as a gallery.

As always, the universe seems to reflect the need at hand. Photography is ruled by Pisces and Neptune, with Uranus and Mercury as secondary rulers. Mercury here rules the Ascendant and is appropriately positioned in Pisces in the vocation/career tenth house. Uranus, the secondary ruler of photography, is in the ninth house of travel in trine to the Ascendant. This placement was chosen to support his desire to travel around the world. The Sun, Mars, and Jupiter in the house of money from career resonate with his desire to explore new horizons and make a living at the same time. Jupiter is the natural ruler of travel, and co-rules the election tenth house of his vocation. Mars is the natural

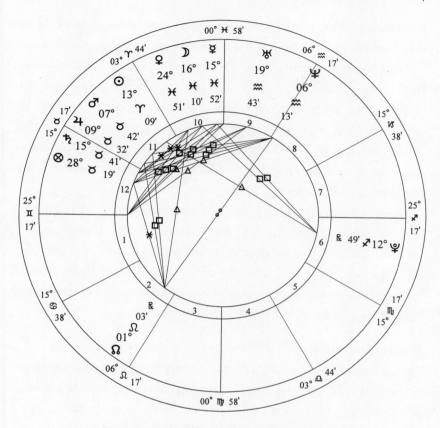

Business Election Chart II—Photography Studio
April 2, 2000 / 10:23 AM EDT / Manhattan, New York
Placidus Houses

ruler of adventure, and co-rules the election sixth house of work. Mars also rules the eleventh house of one's wishes, and the business income.

The Sun is the natural ruler of enjoyment, and rules the election third house of communication. The client communicates through his photography. The Moon is cooperating with a conjunction to Venus in the tenth house of fame. Venus rules all creative endeavors, and is the ruling planet of the election fifth house of creativity. The Moon conjunct Venus adds the benefit of public awareness, and the client is indeed sought after for his fine photography.

Neptune is in the eighth house and conjunct the cusp of the ninth, so it influences both houses. The eighth house shows income from the public and others in general, so we can conclude that his photography offers income, and travel. The end of the matter is shown by fourth-house ruler Mercury in Pisces applying to sextile Saturn, thus providing the opportunity for a long and successful career.

Election for Business III—Daycare

The client had been running a daycare service from her home for over a year and was doing so well that she decided to open a daycare business in her hometown. Leo, the sign ruling children, is at the Midheaven. The planets Mars, Mercury, and the Sun are strongly situated in the tenth house of business. As mentioned previously, Mars in the tenth house is especially good for business. It lends the impetus and drive to succeed. Here it furnishes an added benefit as co-ruler of the Scorpio Ascendant, thus connecting the client with the business. It also defines the client as someone who has a great deal of energy and ambition.

The Sun, the natural ruler of children, in the tenth house is quite favorable for this particular business. Work that involves children is co-ruled by the Moon, and here the Moon is aptly placed in the fifth house of children. She first applies to a sextile with Jupiter in the election eighth house of money from others. Since Jupiter rules the election sec-

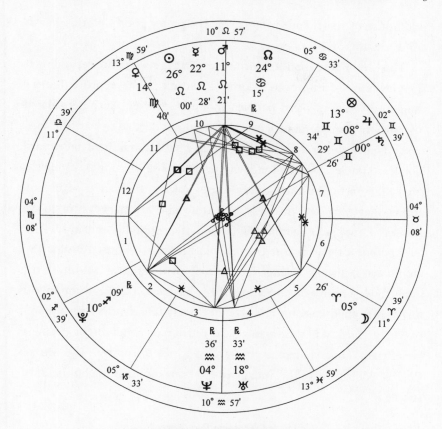

Business Election Chart III—Daycare
August 18, 2000 / 12:00 PM EDT / Nyack, New York
Placidus Houses

ond house of the client's money, this is a pretty good sign that her income will improve.

The Moon next applies to trine Pluto in the second house, adding to the likelihood of improved income as a result of this venture. Pluto is the natural ruler of other people's money. However, Pluto here also illustrates the considerable personal investment needed to start this business. Over time, though, it will result in a substantial financial reward. The fixed angles give the longevity needed. The Moon next applies to trine Mars in the business tenth house, linking the planets of income and money with the business. We were able to place Venus in the eleventh house, adding to the likelihood of a profitable endeavor.

The end of the matter is shown in the fourth house. Ordinarily I would avoid placing Uranus on the cusp of this house. However, it is perfectly descriptive of the nature of her business. There is a continuous turnover as children come and go. They rarely spend more than a year or two in her facility. In this instance, the retrograde condition of Uranus is beneficial. While change is constant, it is not disruptive. The Moon's final aspect, a trine to the Sun, gives the assurance that the business will succeed.

Election for Business IV—Astrology Business

Although this is a business election, it also falls into the category of a personal service. The election was done for an astrologer friend of mine who wanted to build an astrology business of her own. Aquarius and Uranus rule astrology and astrologers, so we chose to place Aquarius at the Midheaven. Venus, ruling the election sixth house of work and service, is well placed in the career tenth house. She is conjunct the planet ruling astrology. The Ascendant is equally important, as this is very much a personal endeavor. Here, Mercury, ruling the Ascendant, is placed in the public seventh house, and is also conjunct the eighth-house cusp. Mercury is in mutual reception with Jupiter conjunct the first. Jupiter rules the seventh house of the public and others in general.

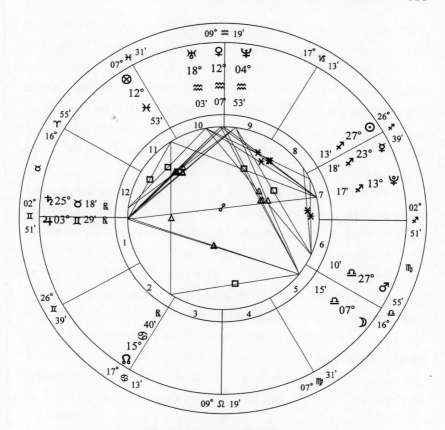

Business Election Chart IV—Astrology Business
December 18, 2000 / 2:52 PM EST / Manhattan, New York
Placidus Houses

The mutual reception between these two planets enables each one to operate equally well in either house of the chart. Here we have the planet ruling the astrologer and the planet ruling her potential clients in a cooperative arrangement. It further illustrates that the exchange between astrologer and client will be mutually beneficial. Jupiter, also ruling the eighth house of their money, affirms the likelihood of ample payment for services rendered. The Sun posited in the eighth house supports this conclusion.

Pluto in the seventh house, in this instance, is aptly descriptive of those with problems or concerns who come to an astrologer for guidance. Often doctors and other health care professionals have an angular Pluto in their natal chart. In an election chart, it describes the area where you will transform others or be transformed. Interestingly, Pluto disposed by Jupiter in mutual reception with Mercury hints at the reform promised, which is a result of the rapport between client and astrologer.

The Moon in Libra is supportive of working with others. She is placed in the fifth house of creativity in the election chart. Her many aspects, all positive, promise lots of activity and a vigorous approach to her practice. Together with Mercury, she describes the client as someone with many talents and interests. The Moon first applies to trine Venus, ruling the election sixth house. This contact shows that the client's work and career are interchangeable. The Moon applies to favorable aspects with all the planets including a trine to Uranus, the natural ruler of astrology, thus enabling the client to carry out her objective. In this instance, Uranus in the tenth house aptly describes her unusual choice of profession. The Moon's final aspect, a sextile to the Sun, supports the client's desire to do the work she loves. The Sun, just sextile to Mars in the house of work, upholds this judgment. The Sun also rules the end of the matter, and provides further validation.

ELEVENTH-HOUSE ELECTIONS

The eleventh house is considered when organizing a fellowship, frater-
nity, lodge, brotherhood, civic group, or any cooperative group. It is important when creating a center where people can come together and
share similar interests. Any group or club consisting of a membership
falls into the eleventh house. It is also considered when applying for
membership or admittance to a private club.

Election to Organize a Group

The creation of a center that is not for profit and has a membership is
ruled by the eleventh house. If the center is intended to be a business
venture for profit, it becomes a tenth-house matter. With most clubs or
groups, the membership is intended to sustain the group, so to increase
the number of members, place Jupiter in the eleventh house. Saturn
and Uranus are the natural rulers of group activity. Venus is also considered because it is the natural ruler of social functions and gatherings.
When joining any club, fellowship, society, or cooperative group, look
for easy aspects between the ruler of the first house, the Moon, and the
planet ruling the eleventh house. Try to keep the more troublesome
planets out of the eleventh house, and also out of the end-of-the-matter
fourth house, if you want the group to have longevity. The ruler of the
eleventh house in a fixed sign also supports a long life.

The client wanted a good date to initiate the first meeting of what
she hoped would be the beginning of a local astrology group. The time
was selected for the initial meeting, which would take place in her home.
There was no intention to formalize it at the time, so the primary intent
was to attract members, create an interest in the study of astrology, and
draw stimulating people to contribute to the group. The stellium of
planets in the eleventh house should accomplish the objective. Each
planet describes something about the group. Mercury, ruling the Ascendant, is conjunct the cusp of the eleventh house. It describes the
founder as someone who wants to teach and communicate her interest

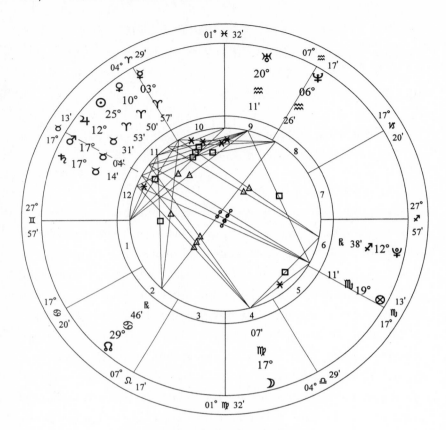

Organize Group Election Chart
April 15, 2000 / 9:33 AM EDT / Lake George, New York
Placidus Houses

to others. Venus, the natural ruler of money, adds the needed financial element to carry the group. Here, it rules the election fifth house, lending an air of creativity and fun.

The Sun is exalted in Aries, and adds vitality to the group. It rules the election third house of learning. Jupiter ruling the election seventh house of the public is sure to increase membership in the group. It also co-rules the election tenth house of success, and is a pretty good indication that the group will flourish. As an added benefit, Jupiter is the natural ruler of excellence in education, so the client should be able to fulfill her wish of teaching astrology. The sign Aries on the eleventh-house cusp describes the psychological makeup of the group. We can be sure it will be a lively, active, and adventurous group. They will have the courage to break down barriers and undertake new initiatives. Mars is strong in Taurus and is conjunct Saturn for longevity, though Saturn is in the next house. Uranus, planet of astrology, is strong in its own sign. It is receiving mixed aspects, descriptive of inherent changes associated with this type of organization. Uranus in the ninth house, though, is particularly supportive of advanced education in astrology.

The Moon is applying to trine Saturn, the natural ruler of organized groups. The Moon aligned with Saturn gives endurance, and together with five planets in fixed signs, enables the group to continue. The mutable angles add the flexibility needed for prolonged growth.

Election to Apply for Membership

An election to apply for membership or acceptance into a private club, group, or organization is also an eleventh-house matter. The important time is when the application for membership is submitted. If done by mail, use the time when it is dropped into the mailbox. The natural rulers of the eleventh house, Saturn and Uranus, should be well aligned with the first-house ruler and the Moon. The planet Mercury is a consideration if one has to complete a membership application, and should be well aligned with the other significators. A benefic in the first house

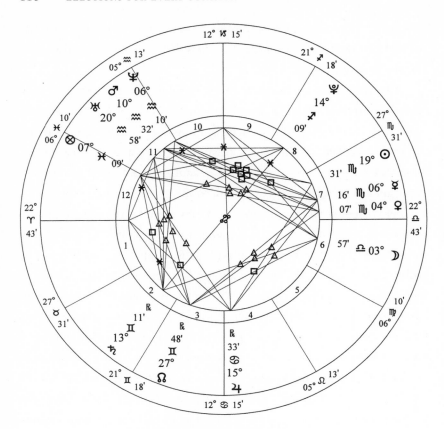

Apply for Membership Election Chart
November 11, 2001 / 3:25 PM EST / Manhattan, New York
Placidus Houses

or favorably aspecting the Ascendant is helpful to the applicant. If possible, the planet ruling the tenth house of success should be brought into the mix.

Here is an example of a straightforward matter and the ease with which the election fulfills the objective. The client wanted to join a private club for the purpose of bringing more business into his firm. Therefore, placing the Moon in the sixth house of work seemed appropriate. Mars in Aquarius, the sign of group endeavors, rules the client. The eleventh house defines the club, with Aquarius on the cusp. The planets Neptune, Mars, and Uranus in the eleventh house characterize the group as an unusual mix of highly motivated, intellectual, and creative people, among whom the client should feel right at home.

The Moon in the cardinal sign of Libra is applying to trine all the air planets in the eleventh house, including Uranus, ruling the club. This is a good indication that the client's membership will be accepted with little resistance. The Moon will also trine Saturn, ruling the tenth house of success, giving the confirmation we need. Although the Moon will square Jupiter, this is not enough to interfere with the application process. Jupiter is not directly tied to the houses in question. The planets Saturn and Mars are mutually applying to a trine aspect. This adds to the likelihood of success in the matter. Saturn not only rules the house of success, but is also co-ruler of the eleventh house of clubs.

The planet Mercury is considered because the client had to fill out some paperwork before meeting with the board. Mercury is square to Mars and Neptune in the eleventh house. At first glance this might raise a red flag. However, Mercury's conjunction with Venus describes his application as impressive. Both Mercury and Venus are disposed by Mars and Pluto in sextile aspect. This indicates that any questions about the application itself will be resolved. Further, Mercury is applying to trine lucky Jupiter in the end-of-the-matter fourth house, and confirms a positive outcome. The Moon, ruling the end of the matter, supports this conclusion with her final aspect, a trine to Uranus.

TWELFTH-HOUSE ELECTIONS

The twelfth house is considered when confinement, voluntary or not, is a probability. This can include entering a hospital, health center, private clinic, treatment center, rest home, nursing home, or other institution. Self-imposed withdrawal comes under the auspices of the twelfth house; for instance, entering a monastery or convent or simply withdrawing for the purpose of one's work. Writers and artists who spend many solitary hours at their craft fall into this category.

Election to Enter a Rehabilitation Facility

The primary objectives here are for successful treatment and to regain one's optimum health. The aspects between the planet ruling the first house, the Moon, and the planets ruling the twelfth and sixth houses should be positive. The Sun and Mercury, the natural rulers of vitality and health, should be well aligned with the Moon and the Ascendant ruler. For added strength and stamina, Mars in good alignment with the above-mentioned planets is certainly a plus. Strengthen the first house by placing a benefic there whenever possible, or place the Moon in its sign of dignity or exaltation. Avoid any difficult aspects from Saturn to the primary rulers, and keep the stressful planets away from the angles.

The client, a distraught mother, contacted me to select a date to admit her son to a rehabilitation facility. Her son had been suffering from a drug-related problem and was now ready to seek help. Our main objective was to give the young man every advantage in his attempt to regain his health. In this instance, it was necessary to link the election chart with the client's birth chart, and specifically with her fifth house of children. She has Cancer on her fifth-house cusp, so the time selected places Cancer on the election Ascendant. The Moon in Leo is in mutual reception with the Sun in the twelfth house of the rehab facility. Any planet or luminary in mutual reception bestows a great deal of latitude upon the person it represents because the planet can be read in its own sign, where it operates best.

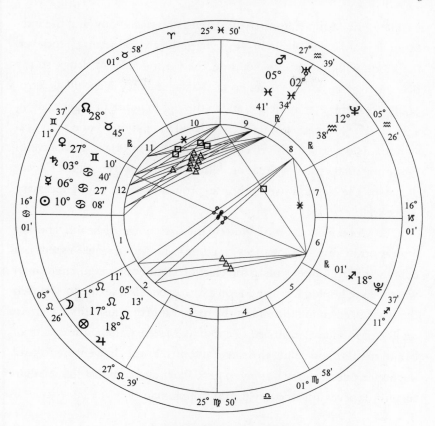

Enter Rehab Election Chart

July 2, 2003 / 6:00 AM EDT / Ossining, New York

Placidus Houses

Here, the Moon rules the young man's physical body, and the indication is that he will regain his strength in the clinical setting. However, the Moon will first oppose Neptune, the natural ruler of drugs, so the first order of business is to let go of the dependency. Neptune is retrograde, weakening its influence, and in the eighth house of regeneration, a good sign. The planet Mars is considered in relation to one's physical stamina. Here, it is in the election ninth house in Pisces, indicative of the young man's current situation. However, Mars is trine all the Cancer planets in the election twelfth house, providing the strength necessary to get well.

The Moon will next trine Pluto in the sixth house of health, another indication of dramatic changes to come. The Moon's next aspect is a conjunction to Jupiter, ruling the election sixth house, confirmation of what we are hoping for. The Moon's final aspect is a sextile to Venus in the twelfth, co-ruling the end-of-the-matter fourth house. If we were to read the Moon in Cancer, she is conjunct Mercury, the natural ruler of health matters and ruling the election fourth house. If we were to read the Sun in Leo, it too will apply to trine Pluto and conjunct Jupiter, confirming a successful recovery for the young man.

A GOOD ELECTION IS A GOOD ELECTION

Sometimes you have the luxury of selecting an election date weeks or even months in advance of the planned event. Once you have a near-perfect election date in hand, you can use it for more than one event simply by rotating the wheel. Here is an example of just such a chart. The date was originally selected for a client's business several weeks in advance of the planned grand opening. By rotating the wheel and shifting the focus to the twelfth house, I was able to use the same date for a client who needed to enter the hospital to undergo tests.

Election to Enter the Hospital

Eliminating an emergency situation, one may enter the hospital for various reasons such as to have elective surgery, to give birth, to go through treatment, or to undergo tests. The purpose of the hospital stay will determine the planets and houses involved. Since we are always concerned with protecting the client's health, avoid any difficult aspects between the primary rulers and the planets Saturn and Neptune.

With this type of an election, the main objectives are to help the client remain healthy or regain optimum health, avoid unnecessary health risks, and ensure a trouble-free experience. The aspects between the planet ruling the first house, the Moon, and the planets ruling the twelfth and sixth houses should be positive. If the hospital visit involves surgery, we want easy aspects between the rulers of the first, twelfth, and eighth houses of the election. Mars should be strong and in good alignment with the above-mentioned planetary rulers. If the hospital visit is for the purpose of undergoing tests, consider Mercury and the ruler of the sixth house. The Sun and Mercury, the natural rulers of vitality and health, should be well aligned with the Moon and the Ascendant ruler. It is always a good idea to strengthen the first house whenever possible. Try to place a benefic conjunct its cusp, or in easy aspect to the Ascendant or its ruler.

In some instances, one may enter the hospital with a preselected date to give birth. This most often occurs when labor is induced or when it is necessary to undergo birth by cesarean section. The latter is a surgical procedure, so the planet ruling the eighth house of surgery should be well aligned with the rulers of the twelfth house, the Ascendant, and the Moon. The natural rulers of surgery, Mars and Pluto, should be strong and in easy aspect with the other significators. Childbirth is ruled by the Moon and is shown in the fifth house. The fifth house or its ruler should be favorably linked with the other significators in the matter. Benefics in the twelfth house are considered protective, particularly Venus and Jupiter.

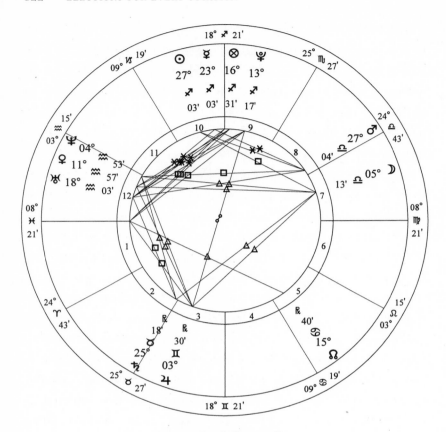

Enter Hospital Election Chart
December 18, 2000 / 11:15 AM EST / New York, New York
Placidus Houses

The client had to enter the hospital for some exploratory tests, so this election is less complicated than it might have been if surgery were involved. The election time should correspond with the hospital admittance. If it involves completing some necessary paperwork, then the beginning of that process is the elected time. The client is represented by Pisces on the Ascendant, with Neptune strongly placed in its natural twelfth house. Neptune is trine to Jupiter, the traditional ruler of Pisces, in the election third house of tests. Although Jupiter is retrograde, it is in mutual reception with Mercury, the natural ruler of both the testing process and health-related matters. The mutual reception indicates adaptability and flexibility related to the matter at hand. However, the retrograde condition of Jupiter in the testing third house hints at the likelihood that more tests will be needed at a later time.

The hospital is known as a prestigious institution, and many of the doctors who practice there are the best in their field. Aquarius on the twelfth-house cusp with Uranus in its own sign supports this reputation. Venus in the twelfth house in wide conjunction with Neptune is a protective influence, but also speaks of the hospital's fine reputation. Interestingly, because Venus rules the election eighth house of hidden matters and the election third house of tests, we can conclude that the tests will likely uncover something that is concealed. It is also possible that what is uncovered will indicate the need for surgery.

The Moon, co-ruling the client, is making only positive applying aspects. However, because she is in an early degree and will make many aspects, we can assume that much will take place before a conclusion is reached. Her final aspect, a conjunction to Mars in the eighth house of surgery, again hints at the possibility that the client may have to undergo a surgical procedure. If so, we can elect another time for the actual surgery. The tests, however, will be conclusive, as evidenced by the election chart.

It turned out that the client did require a surgical procedure and decided to remain in the hospital to have it done immediately. Therefore, the current election would be relevant. The Moon applying to only positive aspects, and Mars strongly positioned in the eighth house of surgery, enabled me to support his decision. Mars received only three applying aspects: a sextile from the Sun, a sextile from Mercury, and the applying conjunction of the Moon. This, together with Venus, the dispositor of Mars, in a grand trine alignment with the planets ruling the client, was confirmation of a successful outcome.

CONCLUSION

In selecting an appropriate election date for the matter at hand, it is helpful to keep in mind the planets ruling the matter. If the natural rulers of a matter are not cooperating, use whatever planets are in good alignment, and make them the significators of the matter. You can always use the Moon as co-ruler of the first-house person, and look for positive applying aspects to the ruler of the house in question.

The Moon is always the primary significator. Therefore, look for days when she is free from difficult aspects. A quick glance at an ephemeris will help pinpoint days when these alignments are present, and then it is simply a matter of working with the election wheel to get the planets where you want them.

Try to strengthen the house of the electional matter in whatever way you can. Also, remember the nature of the signs on the angles of the election chart. While fixed signs may be appropriate for certain endeavors, cardinal and mutable signs are suitable for others. The nature of the matter at hand will help define your choices, and if the endeavor is valid, the universe will mirror it perfectly.

There is no contradiction between the desires of any individual and the ability of the universe to fulfill them. Electional astrology enables us to take advantage of those rare moments in time when everything is in perfect alignment to support the outcome we want. A very good practice is to keep an accurate record of significant events. If you examine the charts for these events, you will always see the correlation in the astrological symbolism. The practice of election is the same process, only it is a preview of the event. On those rare occasions when you are able to achieve a near-perfect election, it is like getting in alignment with the power of the universe and flowing with it. It is a most exhilarating experience.

appendix a

PRINCIPAL HORARY RULERSHIPS

The rulerships in electional astrology have their origins in horary astrology. Included here is an appendix of principal horary rulerships for the interest of the reader in identifying the correspondence between the two approaches.

PRINCIPAL HORARY RULERSHIPS OF THE HOUSES

First House   Questions that are strictly about personal matters, such as health, a change in appearance, a personal enterprise, or the start of something new are answered in the first house. It is the body of the person and everything that involves his well-being.

Second House   Questions about personal possessions, earning capacity, wealth, valuables, and assets are answered here. The second house defines all moveable possessions, such as fine art, jewelry, or antiques, as opposed to fixed possessions, such as land. It also addresses the future.

Third House	Questions about relatives and those in our neighborhood or surroundings are answered in the third house. It answers questions about teachers (elementary education), exams, and basic schooling. It also describes short trips, and travel by automobile or other ground vehicles.
Fourth House	Questions about home, property, land, and buildings are answered in the fourth house. It defines family matters, parents, heredity, and inheritance from family. It is the end of the matter and will have a bearing on the way a horary question turns out. If something is lost, the fourth house shows whether it can be recovered.
Fifth House	Questions about anything that is speculative or a matter of chance, such as betting and gambling, are answered here. The fifth house defines love affairs, recreational interests, and pleasurable pursuits. It answers questions about children and things related to them, including pregnancy. Queries about talent and creativity are answered here.
Sixth House	Questions about routine work, voluntary service, and labor are answered in the sixth house. It defines laborers, workmen, and people who provide a service, as well as employees. In health-related matters, it answers questions about illness and care. It is also relevant in questions about pets and small animals.
Seventh House	Questions about marriage, business and personal partnerships, and contracts with others are answered here. All questions about another person, if the person is not known by the querent, fall into the seventh house. Queries about lawsuits or the dissolution of a partnership fall here.

Eighth House	Queries concerning financial settlements, pensions, insurance benefits, money owed, and taxes are answered in the eighth house. It is also relevant in questions about surgery, retirement, legacies, and death. The eighth house is the money of the marriage partner, and is considered in questions about alimony or any allowance.
Ninth House	Questions about distant travel, relocating to another country, and going away to college are answered here. The ninth house is relevant in matters pertaining to examinations, ceremonies, and religious functions. It answers queries about publishers, educators (professors, mentors, etc.), and attorneys, and is considered when seeking licensing or certification.
Tenth House	Questions about career, business matters, the employer, boss, or authority are answered in the tenth house. It is considered in evaluating the success of anything, and in particular personal honors and reputation. Queries about vocational aptitude and life direction can be seen in the tenth house.
Eleventh House	Questions about career earnings, memberships, and friendships are answered here. As the eighth house from the fourth house of family, the eleventh house answers questions about the death of a parent or family member. Queries concerning anything intangible like hopes and wishes are answered here.
Twelfth House	Questions about confinement, imprisonment, suicide, or any misfortune are answered here. The twelfth house is considered in evaluating anything that requires a solitary, secret, or concealed strategy, such as an undercover operation. It answers questions about hidden enemies or clandestine relationships.

PRINCIPAL HORARY RULERSHIPS OF THE PLANETS
AS SIGNIFICATORS OF PEOPLE AND PLACES

♂♈︎♏︎   Mars describes a person who is young, courageous, and self-reliant, and who possesses a positive personality. It describes a dynamic person, and one who is willing and ready to take on a challenge. With Mars as significator, the person may be argumentative or angry.

Mars describes places where action takes place, such as a sports arena, gymnasium, basketball court, or football field. It also defines places where you may find sharp precision instruments, knives, and scalpels, such as an operating room, dentist's office, or slaughterhouse.

♀♉︎♎︎   Venus describes a person who is interested in balance, equal rights, and social standing, and who is often a romantic. It describes a person who is poised, refined, and kindhearted. Venus as significator describes a person who aspires to the finer things in life.

Venus describes places of entertainment, such as theaters and concert halls, and places of beauty, such as a magnificent garden or superb art gallery. Venus as significator defines places of extravagance, like a fine-jewelry store or an expensive hotel suite.

☿♊︎♍︎   Mercury describes people who are versatile, intelligent, and able to do more than one thing at a time. It defines those who may be indecisive or nervous, or who need to gather a lot of information before

making a decision. Mercury as significator is someone who is in interested in the details.

Mercury describes places of business or where work
is done, such as an office or boardroom. It defines
the place as being full of activity, hectic, and where
information is being exchanged, such as a publishing house or newsroom. Mercury as significator can
mean places of transportation, like a bus terminal
or railway station.

☽♋

The Moon describes those who are nurturing and
supportive of others and are usually quite sensitive.
She describes a person who is quite capable of handling many changes, and is willing to work behind
the scenes and for the benefit of another. The
Moon as significator defines one who has strong
maternal instincts and a need to protect others.

The Moon describes places where people reside,
like an apartment, house, trailer, motor home, or
condominium. The Moon as significator defines
places near or on the water, such as marinas, docks,
piers, and seaports. The Moon rules places where
boats are kept, and watery places such as ponds,
lakes, and reservoirs.

☉♌

The Sun describes people who make an impression
and who are in a strong position. It often defines
one who is influential and respected, and who may
be self-indulgent. The Sun as significator indicates a
person who is willing to take a risk, but may be
somewhat extravagant.

The Sun describes places that are impressive and usually grandiose, such as a palatial estate, a mansion, or a beautiful building. It defines places where people go to have fun, like a resort, gambling casino, or luxurious hotel. The Sun as significator defines places that are costly to maintain or to experience.

♃♐♓

Jupiter defines people who are generous and often philanthropic. They are intellectual, altruistic, and interested in spiritual growth. Jupiter as significator describes a person who is principled, trustworthy, and always willing to be fair. It describes a person who is well educated and interested in educational and legal matters.

Jupiter describes places where people go to learn, like libraries, colleges, and universities, and places where the law is enforced, like courthouses. It defines religious institutions, churches, cathedrals, temples, and places of spiritual learning like a seminary or monastery. Jupiter as significator describes a large building with acreage and an expansive view.

♄♑♒

Saturn as significator describes those who are older, wise, and serious by nature. It defines someone who is cautious and conservative and may want to take control. Saturn describes a person who can be problematic or dependable and reliable, depending on the aspects to it. If well aligned, it describes someone who will stand by you.

Saturn describes places that are old, such as ancient ruins, and places that are lonely and deserted, like an abandoned building, city, or cemetery. It rules any place that is isolated or instills a feeling of melancholy or solitude, like an old cave in the side of a mountain. It describes anything that acts like a barrier, such as a fence, wall, cage, or prison bars.

♅♒ Uranus as significator describes those who are eccentric in some way, but also inventive, creative, and original. It defines people who want to improve upon the status quo, and may do so by challenging existing rules. It describes someone who is likely to stir things up and rearrange matters, usually for the benefit of everyone involved.

Uranus describes places where a great deal of excitement and activity ensues, usually around the latest technology, like the trading floor of the New York Stock Exchange, a television studio, or a scientific laboratory. It defines places of instability where uncontrollable change is likely, such as a hurricane region, flood zone, or tornado valley.

♆♓ Neptune describes people who are creative, sensitive, idealistic, and often vague about their intentions. When Neptune is the significator, it defines a person who is quite intuitive, imaginative, and sometimes deceptive. This is a person who is unwilling to be pinned down, who likes to evade the issue, and who is not telling the whole story.

Neptune defines places of limited mobility, confinement, or restraint, like a hospital, rest home, nursing home, prison, or institution. It describes places that are near the water or prone to flooding, but there is usually something mysterious about the place. It may appear to be more desirable than it actually is. Neptune rules illusion and blurs the issue.

♇♏

Pluto describes people who are secretive, provocative, and manipulative, and who seek power. They may be doctors, surgeons, lawyers, or criminals. When Pluto is the significator, it defines someone who usually does not reveal his intentions and may have another agenda. It describes those who will force changes and may do so violently.

Pluto describes places of devastation and destruction, like a war zone or an earthquake region. It defines places where things are hidden from view, like underground passageways, tunnels, or bunkers. Pluto as significator defines places of death and revival, such as a hospital emergency room, morgue, or crematory.

ALPHABETICAL LIST OF
ELECTIONAL HOUSE RULERSHIPS

A

achievement	tenth house
acquaintances	eleventh house
action	first house
advanced education	ninth house
advancement	tenth house
adventure	first house
advertising, long-range	ninth house
advertising, short-range	third house
agents	third house
agreements	third house
air travel	ninth house

alimony	eighth house
alliances	seventh house
amusements	fifth house
ancestry	fourth house
animals, large	ninth house
animals, small	sixth house
announcements	third house
apartments	fourth house
apparel	second house
appearance	first house
architects	sixth house
artistic ability	fifth house
aspirations	eleventh house
assets	second house
attainment	tenth house
attitudes, one's	first house
attorneys	ninth house
aunts	sixth house
authorities	tenth house
authors	third house
automobiles	third house
automobile trips	third house
awards	tenth house

B

banquets	fifth house
bankruptcy	eighth house

banks	second house
benefactor	ninth house
betting	fifth house
births	fifth house
boating	third house
body, one's	first house
books	third house
books, religious	ninth house
bosses	tenth house
broadcasting	third house
brokers	third house
brotherhoods	eleventh house
brothers	third house
brothers-in-law	ninth house
budgets	second house
buildings	fourth house
burial, one's	fourth house
business	tenth house
business income	eleventh house
business losses	ninth house
business partners	seventh house
buyers	third house

C

card games	fifth house
career, one's	tenth house
cars	third house

cash	second house
casinos	fifth house
cats	sixth house
ceremonies	ninth house
chairmen of the board	tenth house
chance, games of	fifth house
character, one's	first house
charitable institutions	twelfth house
charity	twelfth house
checks	second house
chief executives	tenth house
children	fifth house
churches	ninth house
church affairs	ninth house
cinemas	fifth house
circuses	fifth house
civic groups	eleventh house
civil service	sixth house
clairvoyance	twelfth house
clandestine matters	twelfth house
classmates	third house
clergy	ninth house
clients	seventh house
clothing	sixth house
club members	eleventh house
clubs	eleventh house
coins	second house

collection of debt	eighth house
collectors, tax	eighth house
colleges	ninth house
commendations	ninth house
commerce, international	ninth house
commerce, interstate	ninth house
communication, distant	ninth house
communication, local	third house
communities	eleventh house
community standing, one's	tenth house
competitors	seventh house
complexion, one's	first house
compromise	seventh house
computers	third house
concealment	twelfth house
conception	fifth house
concert halls	fifth house
concerts	fifth house
conclusion of matter	fourth house
confidential matters	twelfth house
confinement	twelfth house
contests, competitive	seventh house
contracts	seventh house
contracts, signing	third house
conventions	eleventh house
convents	twelfth house
conversation	third house

coordination, one's	first house
copyrights	ninth house
correspondence	third house
counselors	ninth house
counselors, group of	eleventh house
countries, foreign	ninth house
court, judge of	tenth house
court, jury of	seventh house
courts of law	ninth house
cousins	third house
co-workers	sixth house
craftsmen	sixth house
creative abilities	fifth house
creativity	fifth house
credentials	ninth house
currency	second house
customers	seventh house

D

dance halls	fifth house
daughters	fifth house
daughters-in-law	eleventh house
dealings with the public	seventh house
death, matters pertaining to	eighth house
debts, personal	second house
debts, recovery of	eighth house
decisions, one's	third house
defendants	seventh house

demeanor, one's	first house
detectives	eighth house
detention	twelfth house
dexterity	third house
dialogue	third house
diet	sixth house
directors	fifth house
discovery	ninth house
disease	sixth house
disguises	twelfth house
disposition, one's	first house
distance	ninth house
distribution	third house
divorce	seventh house
doctors	sixth house
doctors' offices	sixth house
documents, legal	ninth house
documents, signing of	third house
dogs	sixth house
dollars, one's	second house
domestic matters	fourth house
dominant parent	tenth house
donations	ninth house
draftsmen	sixth house
dreams	ninth house
drugs	twelfth house
dwelling, one's	fourth house

E

earning capacity	second house
editors	third house
education, elementary	third house
education, higher	ninth house
employees	sixth house
employers	tenth house
employment	tenth house
end of matter	fourth house
endowments	ninth house
enemies, open	seventh house
enemies, secret	twelfth house
engagement to marry	fifth house
enjoyments	fifth house
entertainment	fifth house
environment, everyday	third house
escape	twelfth house
escrows	eighth house
estates	fourth house
examinations, physical	sixth house
examinations, written	third house
executives	tenth house
exploration	ninth house
exports	ninth house
extended journeys	ninth house
extrasensory perception	twelfth house

F

face	first house
facial features	first house
faith, religious	ninth house
falsehoods	twelfth house
fame	tenth house
famous persons	tenth house
family, one's	fourth house
farms	fourth house
father, one's	tenth house
feet	twelfth house
fellowships	eleventh house
films	fifth house
finances, joint	eighth house
finances of business	eleventh house
finances, personal	second house
financial organizations	eighth house
formal ceremonies	ninth house
forms, business	third house
fraternities	eleventh house
fraud	twelfth house
friends	eleventh house
fun	fifth house
funds, public	eighth house

G

gains, financial	second house
gains from partner	eighth house
gains from public	eighth house
gambling	fifth house
games of chance	fifth house
gardens	fourth house
generative system	eighth house
ghost writers	third house
gifts	second house
giving	second house
goals, one's	tenth house
golf courses	fifth house
government	tenth house
government officials	tenth house
graduation ceremony	ninth house
grandchildren	ninth house
group membership	eleventh house

H

happiness	fifth house
head	first house
healers	sixth house
health, one's	first house
health practitioners	sixth house
heart	fifth house
hidden matters	twelfth house

hidden places	twelfth house
highways	third house
hobbies	fifth house
home, one's	fourth house
home for aged	twelfth house
honors	tenth house
hopes, one's	eleventh house
horses	ninth house
horticulture	sixth house
hospitals	twelfth house
hotels	fourth house
housing, public	fourth house
husband, one's	seventh house
hygiene	sixth house

I

ideals, one's	ninth house
ideas	third house
illness	sixth house
image, one's public	tenth house
immigration	ninth house
impersonators	twelfth house
important people	tenth house
importing	ninth house
imports	ninth house
impression one makes	first house
imprisonment	twelfth house

inauguration ceremony	ninth house
incarnation	first house
income from business	eleventh house
income, one's	second house
income, public	eighth house
information	third house
informers	twelfth house
inheritances	eighth house
inherited tendencies	fourth house
initiatives	first house
in-laws	ninth house
inner development	twelfth house
inquiries	third house
inspectors	sixth house
institutions, charitable	twelfth house
institutions of confinement	twelfth house
institutions of higher learning	ninth house
insurance	eighth house
intellect	third house
international commerce	ninth house
intuitive intellect	ninth house
investments	second house

J

jails	twelfth house
janitors	sixth house
jewelry, one's	second house

journalism	third house
journalists	third house
journeys, long	ninth house
journeys, short	third house
joys, physical	fifth house
joys, spiritual	eleventh house
judges	tenth house
judicial process	ninth house

K

karma	twelfth house
karmic responsibilities	twelfth house
kin	third house
kings	tenth house
kitty	sixth house
knowledge, advanced	ninth house

L

labor	sixth house
labor, gains from	seventh house
laborers	sixth house
land	fourth house
law	ninth house
law, courts of	ninth house
lawsuits	seventh house
lawyers	ninth house
learning	third house

leases	fourth house
leases, signing of	third house
lectures	third house
legacies	eighth house
legal profession	ninth house
legalizing	ninth house
legislation	eleventh house
legislators	eleventh house
letter writing	third house
liabilities	eighth house
libraries	third house
licenses	ninth house
limitations	twelfth house
lotteries	fifth house
love affairs	fifth house
luck	ninth house
lungs	third house

M

magazines	third house
mail	third house
manuscripts	third house
marriage	seventh house
masseurs	sixth house
mate, one's	seventh house
material possessions	second house
matrimony	seventh house

mayors	tenth house
medical professions	sixth house
mediumship	twelfth house
memberships	eleventh house
men of power	tenth house
mental ability	third house
mentality	third house
metaphysics	ninth house
military service	ninth house
mind, higher	ninth house
mind, lower	third house
ministers	ninth house
monasteries	twelfth house
monetary gain from business	eleventh house
monetary gain from profession	eleventh house
monetary gain from real estate	fifth house
money, one's	second house
money from partners	eighth house
money from public	eighth house
mortgages	eighth house
mother, one's	fourth house
motion pictures	fifth house
motoring	third house
music halls	fifth house
mysticism	twelfth house

N

neighborhood	third house
neighbors	third house
nephews	seventh house
newcomer	first house
news	third house
newspapers	third house
nieces	seventh house
nightclubs	fifth house
notoriety, one's	tenth house
novelists	third house
novels	third house
nuns	twelfth house
nunneries	twelfth house
nurses	sixth house
nursing home	twelfth house
nutrition	sixth house

O

obligations	sixth house
occult studies	eighth house
occupation	tenth house
office, high	tenth house
office, home	fourth house
office, one's	sixth house
officials	tenth house
offspring	fifth house

operations	eighth house
opinion, one's	first house
opponents	seventh house
ordainment	ninth house
organizations	eleventh house
orphanages	twelfth house
outcome of the matter	fourth house
outlook, one's	first house
ownership	second house

P

pageants	ninth house
papers	third house
parades	ninth house
parent, least influential	fourth house
parent, most influential	tenth house
parenthood	fifth house
parishes	ninth house
parks	fifth house
Parliament	eleventh house
parties	fifth house
partners	seventh house
past	twelfth house
pastimes	fifth house
patents	ninth house
penitentiaries	twelfth house
pensions	eighth house

people, famous	tenth house
people, strangers	seventh house
perception	third house
periodicals	third house
persecution	twelfth house
personal affairs	first house
personality, one's	first house
petitions	third house
pets, domestic	sixth house
philanthropy	ninth house
philosophy	ninth house
physical body, one's	first house
physicians	sixth house
picnics	fifth house
places, faraway	ninth house
plaintiff	first house
pleasure	fifth house
politics	tenth house
politics, foreign	ninth house
politics, municipal	fourth house
popularity	tenth house
position, one's	tenth house
possessions, one's	second house
possessions of partner	eighth house
post offices	third house
power in society, one's	tenth house

powerful persons	tenth house
preachers	ninth house
pregnancy	fifth house
presidents	tenth house
press	third house
printing	third house
prison	twelfth house
private investigators	twelfth house
profession, money from	eleventh house
profession, one's	tenth house
professional men	tenth house
professors	ninth house
profit and loss	second house
projects, one's	eleventh house
promotions	tenth house
property, income from	fifth house
property, one's	fourth house
prophecy	ninth house
public	seventh house
public appearance, one's	tenth house
public enemies	seventh house
public life	tenth house
publications	third house
publishing	ninth house
purchasing	second house

Q

quarrels	seventh house
querent (horary)	first house
queries	third house
quotations	third house

R

races	fifth house
racing	fifth house
radio broadcasting	ninth house
railway station	third house
rank, one's	tenth house
reading	third house
real estate	fourth house
real estate, income from	fifth house
recreation	fifth house
reformatories	twelfth house
registrars	ninth house
relationships	seventh house
relatives	third house
religion	ninth house
removal	fourth house
rentals	fourth house
reporters	third house
representatives, foreign	ninth house
representatives, one's	seventh house
reputation, one's	tenth house

residence, one's	fourth house
resorts	fifth house
resources, one's	second house
rest home	twelfth house
restrictions	twelfth house
result, end	fourth house
retirement	twelfth house
retreats	twelfth house
revenue, one's	second house
riches	second house
risks	fifth house
rituals	ninth house
rivals	seventh house
roads	third house
romance	fifth house
rooming house	fourth house
rumors	third house

S

saloons	fifth house
sanitariums	twelfth house
scandals	twelfth house
schools, in general	third house
schools of higher learning	ninth house
scientific institutions	ninth house
scientific publications	ninth house
seclusion, places of	twelfth house

secret enemies	twelfth house
secret societies	twelfth house
secrets	twelfth house
securities	second house
security, one's	fourth house
seers	twelfth house
self	first house
self-destruction	twelfth house
self-expression	fifth house
servants	sixth house
service, one's	sixth house
services, military	sixth house
servitude	twelfth house
settlements	seventh house
sewing	sixth house
sexuality	eighth house
shipping	third house
shopkeepers	sixth house
show business	fifth house
sickness	sixth house
signatures	third house
signing papers	third house
simulation	twelfth house
sisters	third house
slaughterhouses	eighth house
social affairs	fifth house
social life, one's	seventh house

social security	eighth house
social service	twelfth house
societies	eleventh house
societies, philosophical	ninth house
societies, secret	twelfth house
society, high	fifth house
society, one's position in	tenth house
solitude, places of	twelfth house
sons	fifth house
sons-in-law	eleventh house
sororities	eleventh house
sorrows	twelfth house
speculation	fifth house
speech	third house
spies	twelfth house
spiritual counselors	twelfth house
spirituality	ninth house
sporting events	fifth house
sports	fifth house
spouse	seventh house
stadiums	fifth house
stage	fifth house
standing, one's	tenth house
starts, one's	first house
stature, one's	first house
status, one's	tenth house
stepchildren, one's	eleventh house

stock investments	second house
stock speculation	fifth house
storekeepers	sixth house
strangers, agreements with	seventh house
streets	third house
students	third house
studies	third house
subordinates, one's	sixth house
success, one's	tenth house
superiors, one's	tenth house
supporters, one's	eleventh house
Supreme Court	ninth house
surgeons	eighth house
surgery	eighth house
sweethearts	seventh house

T

tailors	sixth house
taxes	eighth house
teachers	third house
teachers, college	ninth house
telegrams	third house
telephones	third house
television broadcasting	ninth house
temperament, one's	first house
tenants	sixth house
tendencies, inherent	fourth house

termination of the matter	fourth house
tests, written and oral	third house
theaters	fifth house
thought	third house
thought, abstract	ninth house
trade, foreign	ninth house
trade, local	third house
trade, national	tenth house
traffic	third house
traffic, long-distance	ninth house
trailer houses	fourth house
trains	third house
transit, mass	third house
translators	third house
transportation	third house
transportation, long-distance	ninth house
travel by air	ninth house
travel, local	third house
trials, judicial	ninth house
troubles	twelfth house
trucks	third house
trust funds	eighth house

U

uncles	sixth house
unconscious mind	twelfth house
undertaker	eighth house

undesignated person	seventh house
unemployment	twelfth house
unions	seventh house
universities	ninth house

V

vacations	fifth house
valuables, personal	second house
vehicles	third house
veils	twelfth house
ventures, new	first house
veterinarians	sixth house
visionaries	twelfth house
visitor	third house
vocations	tenth house
voluntary labor	sixth house
voyages	ninth house

W

walking	third house
wallets	second house
wardens	twelfth house
wealth, personal	second house
wealth of partner	eighth house
weddings	seventh house
welfare work	twelfth house
wells	fourth house

widows	twelfth house
wife, one's	seventh house
wills	eighth house
wishes, one's	eleventh house
womb	fourth house
work	sixth house
workers	sixth house
writers	third house
writings, published	ninth house

X

x-ray rooms	twelfth house

Y

yard, one's	fourth house
youngsters	fifth house
youth	fifth house

Z

zenith	tenth house
zoos	sixth house

appendix c

SAMPLE ELECTION CHARTS

The following are election charts I did for clients in 2004, along with commentary.

ADMISSION TO PRIVATE SCHOOL

The client requested a favorable date to apply for her daughter's admission to a private elementary school. Here the Moon rules the third house, representing the school, and will trine the Sun, ruling the client's daughter, in the tenth house of success. The Moon's final aspect is a sextile to Pluto, co-ruler of the seventh house of partnerships. The added benefit of Jupiter in the fifth house secured a positive outcome.

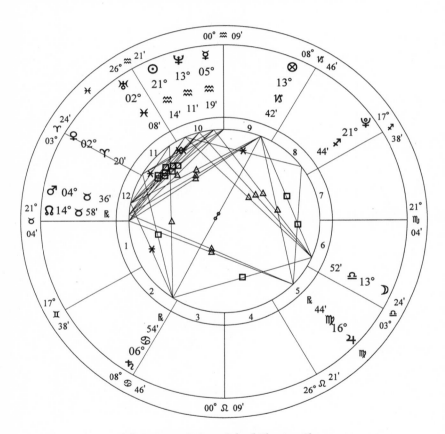

Admission to Private School Election Chart
February 10, 2004 / 10:45 AM EST / Manhattan, New York
Placidus Houses

OPEN BEAUTY SALON

The client was beginning a new business and wanted a good date for
the grand opening. Here the Moon rules the client and is in the tenth
house of success and applying to conjunct Venus, the natural ruler of
the beauty business. Mars in the eleventh of business income in mutual
reception with Venus should stimulate cash flow, and its trine to third-
house Jupiter is an added benefit. The Moon's final aspect is a sextile to
Mercury.

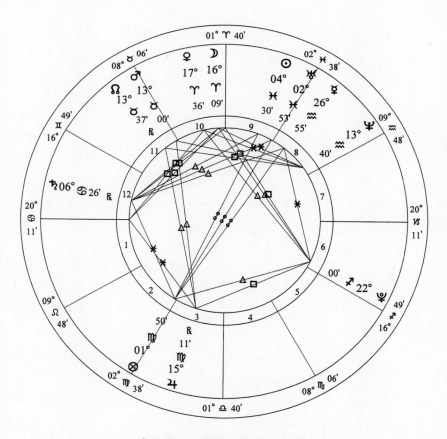

Open Beauty Salon Election Chart
February 23, 2004 / 1:50 PM EST / Manhattan, New York
Placidus Houses

REPEAT LICENSING EXAM

The client, ruled by Mercury retrograde, was repeating an examination to gain her broker's license. Mercury by retrograde motion is applying to sextile Venus, ruling the ninth house of licensing. The Moon is applying to trine Pluto and sextile Mars, both ruling the third house of exams. Jupiter conjunct the Ascendant and trine the ninth-house Sun assures a positive outcome.

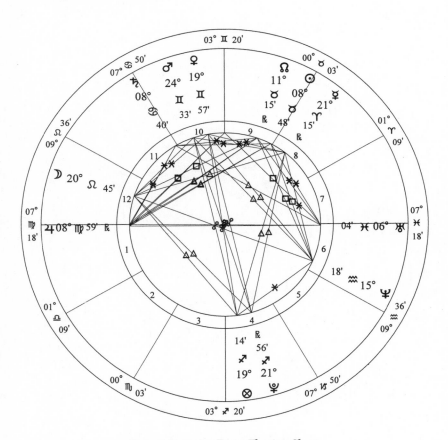

Repeat Licensing Exam Election Chart
April 28, 2004 / 2:33 PM EDT / New York, New York
Placidus Houses

MARRIAGE (SECOND FOR BOTH)

Although marriage is a seventh-house function, a second marriage is shown by the ninth house. Therefore, Mars and Venus, ruling the bride and groom, are placed in the ninth house. The Moon applies favorably to both significators, and her final aspect is a trine to Mars, ruling the marriage seventh house. The Sun and North Node in the seventh add strength to the union. This is not a perfect election because the Sun applies to a square with Neptune. However, the primary significators, Mars, Venus, and the Moon, are well aligned.

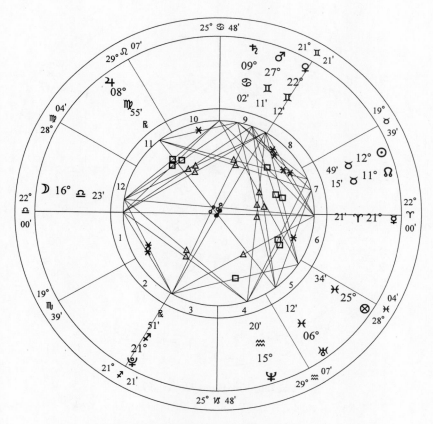

Marriage Election Chart (Second for Both)

May 2, 2004 / 6:02:35 PM EDT / New York, New York

Placidus Houses

MOVE INTO NEW HOME

The client requested a date to move into his new home. Here the Moon makes only one applying aspect, a trine to Mars, ruling the fourth house. The Moon in Libra and Venus conjunct Mars are descriptive of a beautiful home. The fixed angles were chosen for permanence. When moving in, the time should coincide with bringing the first items into the home.

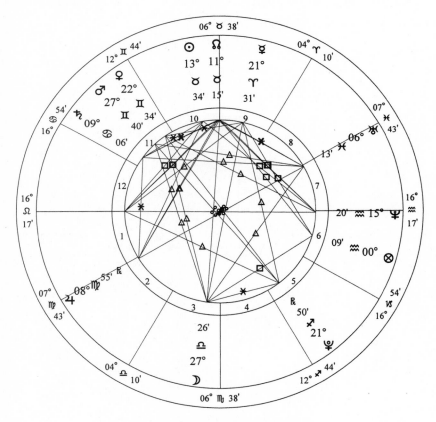

Move into New Home Election Chart
May 3, 2004 / 12:25 PM EDT / Tarrytown, New York
Placidus Houses

JOB INTERVIEW

The client was applying for a position as an investment banker. Therefore, Mercury, ruling him, is placed in the eighth house of shared investments. Mercury is sextile to Venus, the natural ruler of banking, in the tenth house of success, and the Moon applies favorably to both significators. Since Mercury rules both the client and his prospective employer in the election chart, the position is literally a foregone conclusion. Jupiter is conjunct the Ascendant for luck.

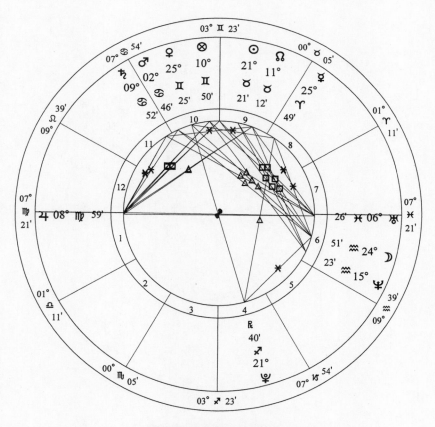

Job Interview Election Chart
May 11, 2004 / 1:42 PM EST / Manhattan, New York
Placidus Houses

RENEGOTIATE INSURANCE CLAIM

The client was not happy with a settlement offered by her insurance company and requested arbitration. This date was chosen to give her the advantage. Retrograde Venus rules both my client and the insurance company. Venus trine the Ascendant together with the Moon's favorable aspects give her the advantage. The Moon's final aspect, a sextile to Pluto, the natural ruler of the eighth house in the client's second house of money, favors a positive outcome.

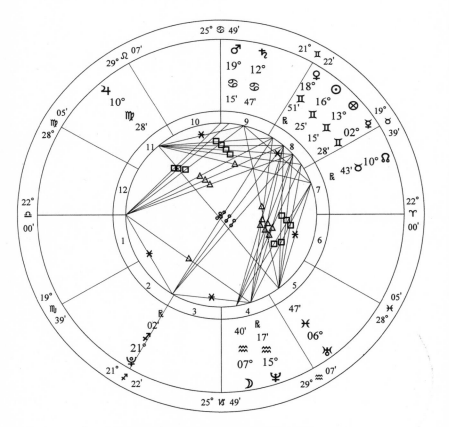

Renegotiate Insurance Claim Election Chart
June 6, 2004 / 3:45 PM EDT / New York, New York
Placidus Houses

OFFER TO PURCHASE HOME

An offer to purchase requires agreement with another party; therefore, the rulers of the first and seventh houses must be in harmony. Here Venus and Mars are sextile, providing the opportunity to negotiate. In this situation the buyer must be connected with the home, and is by way of the Moon, co-ruler of my client applying to sextile Saturn, ruling the house. After some delay, my client's offer was accepted, and he purchased the house.

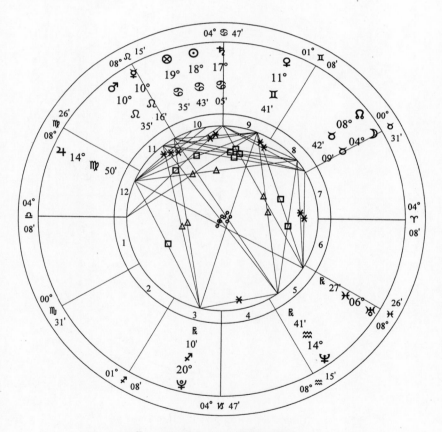

Offer to Purchase Home Election Chart
July 10, 2004 / 12:00 PM EDT / Valley Stream, New York
Placidus Houses

MINOR ELECTIVE SURGERY

This date was chosen to remove an unsightly facial mole, and the procedure was done in the doctor's office. Venus and Mars rule the client and the doctor, respectively, and are in a favorable sextile aspect. Mars, the natural ruler of surgical procedures, is exalted by house. Venus, the natural ruler of beauty, is trine the Ascendant, and the Moon's final aspect is a sextile to Venus.

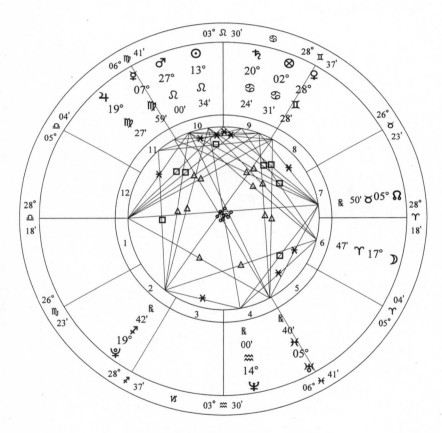

Minor Elective Surgery Election Chart
August 5, 2004 / 12:21 PM EDT / New York, New York
Placidus Houses

SETTLE ESTATE

The client was the executor of his father's estate and wanted to avoid disagreements with other members of the family. We selected this date to facilitate an easy resolution. Saturn, his ruler, posited in the seventh house of agreements indicates his willingness to meet them halfway. The estate is ruled by the Sun and planets in the eighth house. The Moon, ruling the other parties, applies to sextile most of the eighth-house planets and Saturn in the seventh for a favorable final resolution.

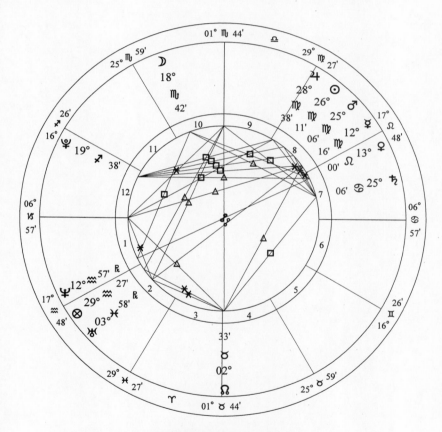

Settle Estate Election Chart
September 18, 2004 / 3:00 PM EDT / Darien, Connecticut
Placidus Houses

appendix d

ONE MORE ELECTION CHART

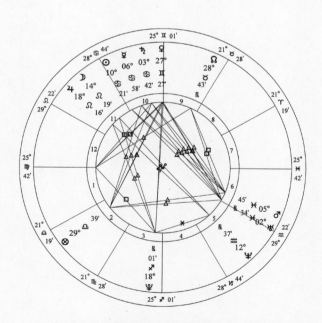

Mail Manuscript to Publisher Election Chart
July 2, 2003 / 11:45 AM EDT / Montauk, New York
Placidus Houses

GLOSSARY

The following is a compilation of principal electional terms. Many of the terms listed in this glossary can be defined in a broader sense. In some instances the same term can have multiple meanings. However, included here are mainly those definitions that apply to electional astrology, and in particular to an election chart.

Accidental Dignity
Strengthening a planet by placing it in an angular house or in the house corresponding to the natural sign it rules. For example, Venus is accidentally dignified in the second or seventh house or in any angular house. Mercury is accidentally dignified in the third or sixth house and in any angular house.

Affinity
The natural compatibility between certain planets and signs. For example, the Moon has a natural affinity with other water planets and signs.

Afflicted

A planet unfavorably aspected, particularly by a malefic planet.

Air Signs

Gemini, Libra, and Aquarius.

Angular Houses

The first, fourth, seventh, and tenth houses. The angular houses are considered the action houses, and planets here tend to operate more quickly.

Applying Aspect

A planet approaching an aspect that is not yet exact.

Ascendant

The Ascendant is also called the rising sign or first-house cusp. It is the degree of the zodiac sign rising on the eastern horizon at the moment of birth. In an election chart it is selected in advance to represent the person initiating action.

Ascendant Ruler

The planet ruling the sign on the first-house cusp.

Aspect

The angular relationship between planets, house cusps, and other points, measured in degrees. For electional purposes, the primary aspects are the conjunction, sextile, square, trine, opposition, parallel, and contraparallel.

Benefic Planet

The planets considered to be fortunate or having a beneficial influence. For electional purposes, they are Venus, Jupiter, and the Sun. The Part of Fortune and the North Node of the Moon are also considered beneficial.

Besieged

A planet is considered besieged when it is between two malefic planets, or when it has separated from one malefic planet and is applying to another.

Cadent Houses

The cadent houses are the third, sixth, ninth, and twelfth. They are behind the angular houses, and planets here are the last to act.

Cardinal Signs

Aries, Cancer, Libra, and Capricorn. The cardinal signs correspond to the angular houses and cardinal points of the compass.

Combust

A planet is considered combust when it is conjunct the Sun or within eight degrees of the Sun. This placement weakens the strength of the planet because it is considered burned up by the Sun's rays. The only exception to this rule is the fire planet Mars, which is considered very strong when conjunct the Sun.

Contraparallel

Two planets are contraparallel when they have the same degree of declination, but one is north and one is south of the celestial equator. Although a minor aspect, it is considered a positive final aspect in an election chart. If the overall chart is strong, the contraparallel means assistance to complete the matter at hand.

Co-ruler

See co-significator.

Co-significator

A planet also ruling a house (co-ruler) either by being situated in the house, or by ruling an intercepted sign within a house. The primary ruler is the planet ruling the sign on the cusp of any house. The Moon is always a co-significator of the first-house person.

Critical Degrees

The degrees in which a planet or luminary is considered weak. For electional purposes, they are 0° and 29°, being at the beginning and end of the sign, respectively; 0° is considered too early and 29° too late.

Cusp

The boundary or dividing line between the houses of the horoscope.

Debility

A planet in a weak position either by sign, house, or aspect. A planet in its sign of detriment or fall is considered weak.

Declination

The angular distance above and below the celestial equator.

Decreasing in Light

The waning phase of the Moon. After she has reached her opposition to the Sun (full Moon), she decreases in light each day until she conjuncts the Sun at the next new Moon.

Detriment

Considered a weak position for a planet, this is the sign opposite the one the planet rules. The Moon is in dignity in Cancer and in detriment in Capricorn.

Dignity

Considered a strong position for a planet, this is the sign the planet rules. The Sun is dignified in Leo, and Venus is dignified in Taurus and Libra.

Direct Motion

The forward motion of the planets through the signs of the zodiac from Aries to Pisces.

Dispositor

A planet is the dispositor of another planet whose sign it occupies. If Mars is in Gemini, its dispositor is Mercury, ruler of Gemini. A planet in its own sign, like Mars in Aries, disposes of itself.

Earth Signs

Taurus, Virgo, and Capricorn.

Eclipse

A solar eclipse is the full or partial obscuring of the Sun by the Moon. A lunar eclipse is the full or partial obscuring of the Moon by the Sun. Neither event is desirable for an electional matter.

Elected Matter

The subject or topic of the election.

Elected Time

The birth time of the electional chart.

Electional Chart

A chart cast to reflect the ideal time to take action to successfully accomplish the intended purpose.

Elements

Fire, earth, air, and water.

Essential Dignity

A planet in the sign of its rulership, such as Mars in Aries.

Exaltation

The sign in which a planet functions at its best. The Moon is exalted in Taurus, and the Sun is exalted in Aries.

Fall

The sign opposite a planet's sign of exaltation. In this position, a planet is considered "ill at ease" or debilitated. The Moon is in its fall in Scorpio. The Sun is in its fall in Aquarius.

Finality

The moment at which you no longer have control of the elected matter. The moment of finality should correspond with the birth time of the election.

Fire Signs

Aries, Leo, and Sagittarius.

Fixed Signs

Taurus, Leo, Scorpio, and Aquarius.

Hindrance

Any obstacle or impediment that interferes with the functioning of a planet.

Horary Chart

A horoscope drawn at the moment a question is posed with the intent of answering the question. Horary, which means "the hour of," is the foundation of electional astrology.

House of the Matter

The house concerned with the primary subject of the elected matter. The objective is to enhance that area of the horoscope.

Impeded

A planet is impeded when it is poorly aspected.

Inconjunct

An aspect of 150° between planets, also called a quincunx. Though not a major aspect, when it occurs in an election chart, and particularly if the Moon is involved, it is necessary to reorganize some piece of the matter.

Increasing in Light

The waxing phase of the Moon. After she has conjuncted the Sun (new Moon), she increases in light each day until she reaches her opposition to the Sun (full Moon).

Intercepted

A sign entirely within a house that does not appear on the cusp. When a planet occupies that sign, it is said to be intercepted. In an election chart, an intercepted planet is somewhat restricted or delayed.

Lunar Eclipse

A lunar eclipse occurs when the earth is between the Moon and the Sun, obscuring the light of the Sun from the Moon. Lunar eclipses are associated with endings and considered unfavorable for electional matters.

Luminaries

The lights—the Sun and Moon.

Major Aspects

The conjunction (0°), sextile (60°), square (90°), trine (120°), and opposition (180°).

Malefic

An adverse planet or one considered troublesome. Saturn, Uranus, Neptune, and Pluto are considered malefic, and also Mars, if badly aspected by one of these.

Midheaven

The high point of the chart, or where the Sun is at noon local time. In electional terms, it corresponds with the tenth house of success.

Moon

The Moon is key in electional astrology because she is always a co-significator of the first-house person who initiates the action, she rules all action to take place, and she brings everything together with her applying aspects. Every aspect the Moon makes has something to say about the unfolding of the electional matter. Therefore, it is beneficial to keep her free from any difficult aspects.

Mutable Signs

Gemini, Virgo, Sagittarius, and Pisces.

Mutual Application

A situation in which two planets are moving toward each other by applying aspect because one is advancing and the other is retrograde.

Mutual Reception

When two planets occupy each other's ruling signs, they are in reception, as with Venus in Aries and Mars in Taurus. This condition allows each planet to change position and lends flexibility to the interpretation of the chart. It is considered a favorable condition, particularly if one of the planets represents a key person in the matter.

Natal Chart

Also called the birth chart, it is a map of the heavens at the moment of one's birth, from an earth perspective.

Natural House

The natural association between the twelve signs of the zodiac and their corresponding houses. Aries is associated with the first house, Taurus the second house, Gemini and third house, and so on. The meaning of the sign corresponds to the natural house. The fourth house is the natural house of family, a Cancerian interest.

Natural Ruler

The accepted subject matter ruled by the planet. The Sun is the natural ruler of men, speculation, and creativity, while the Moon is the natural ruler of women, home, and fluctuation.

Occultation

When the Moon conjuncts another planet or the Sun and also eclipses it by declination. The occulted body is rendered less powerful, and if this occurs in an election chart, the person or matter represented by that body may not prevail.

Orb of Influence

The Moon is allowed all applying aspects in an election chart and is therefore not subject to any orb of influence. However, all other bodies are subject to acceptable orbs between zero and ten degrees applying. The Moon or the planet ruling the election Ascendant should be in a favorable applying aspect with the planet ruling the matter of your election.

Parallel of Declination

When two planets are the same number of degrees north or south of the celestial equator. In electional charts, the parallel acts like a positive conjunction, and when it is the Moon's final aspect, it brings the matter to a favorable conclusion.

Part of Fortune

Considered a benefic point, it is on the ecliptic the same distance from the eastern horizon as the Moon is from the Sun. In electional matters, the Part of Fortune in the house of the matter enhances that house.

Planetary Strength

The power of a planet is evaluated by analyzing the following:

1) its position by sign (dignity, detriment, exaltation, fall)
2) its position by house
3) its alignment to the other planets and points (aspects)

A planet is always strong in its natural house, or in an angular house by accidental dignity. If it is also well placed by sign and aspect, it has planetary strength.

Posited

Posited refers to where a planet is placed in the election chart.

Ptolemaic Aspects

The major aspects as defined by Ptolemy: the conjunction, sextile, square, trine, and opposition.

Qualities

Cardinal, fixed, and mutable.

Querent

A horary term meaning "the person asking the question."

Quesited

A horary term meaning "the person or matter asked about."

Quincunx

A 150° aspect, also called an inconjunct. When it occurs in an election chart, some form of reorganization is required.

Refranation

When a planet, most often the Moon, is applying to an aspect with another planet but is unable to reach it because the planet moves out of the sign before the aspect is completed. This usually occurs when a planet is in the last degrees of a sign and moves to the next sign before the aspect is perfected. For example, the Moon in an early degree of Taurus applying to trine the Sun in a late degree of Capricorn may not be able to reach the Sun before it moves into Aquarius. Depending on the motion of the Moon, whether fast or slow, it may refrain from the aspect. If this occurs in an election chart, something is dropped. Refer to an aspectarian for the Moon's daily motion.

Retrograde

When a planet appears to move backward along the ecliptic in the opposite order of the signs.

Retrograde Application

When two planets are applying to each other to form an aspect while in retrograde motion.

Returning Retrograde

A planet returning by retrograde motion to the sign it occupied previously.

Rising Sign

The degree of the zodiac sign rising on the eastern horizon at the moment of birth, also called the Ascendant. In an election chart, the rising sign is the zodiac degree and sign selected to represent the person initiating action.

Rulerships

The signs, planets, and houses that rule the matter.

Separating Aspect

A planet moving away from the exact aspect.

Significator

A horary term indicating the planet that rules the person or matter of the election. In a business election chart, the planet ruling the tenth-house cusp is referred to as the significator of the business.

Solar Eclipse

A solar eclipse is when the Moon blocks the Sun's light, diminishing its strength. Since the Sun is always important to the success of any elected endeavor, an eclipse should be avoided. An eclipse can bring an unexpected change in direction. Therefore, it is not the most stable environment in which to initiate an election. As a general rule, it is best to wait at least one week before and after an eclipse to take action.

Stellium

A conjunction of three or more planets in the same house or sign in the astrological chart. It indicates a high degree of focus in that area.

Succedent Houses

The succedent houses are the second, fifth, eighth, and eleventh. They are in front of the angular houses, and planets here tend to operate in the immediate future.

Void-of-Course

The Moon is void-of-course when it ceases to form any further aspects before leaving the sign it is in. A planet can also be void-of-course. It remains void until it enters the next sign. Actions taken while the Moon is void-of-course do not turn out as planned or miss the mark of their intended goal.

Waning Moon

Decreasing in light. When the Moon has reached her opposition to the Sun (full Moon), she decreases in light each day until she arrives at her conjunction to the Sun (new Moon). A waning Moon favors completion or minimizing the outcome of the matter. For example, a major purchase made on a waning Moon favors a lower price, and therefore the buyer.

Water Signs

Cancer, Scorpio, and Pisces.

Waxing Moon

Increasing in light. When the Moon moves away from her conjunction to the Sun (new Moon), she increases in light each day until she arrives at her opposition to the Sun (full Moon). A waxing Moon favors growth and is appropriate for a business election or any matter where increase is wanted.

BIBLIOGRAPHY

Arroyo, Stephen. *Astrology, Karma & Transformation*. Vancouver, WA: CRCS Publications, 1978.

Baigent, Michael, Nicholas Campion, and Charles Harvey. *Mundane Astrology*. Wellingborough, Northamptonshire: Aquarian Press, 1984.

Barclay, Olivia. *Horary Astrology Rediscovered*. West Chester, PA: Whitford Press, 1990.

Bills, Rex E. *The Rulership Book*. Richmond, VA: Macoy Publishing & Masonic Supply Co., Inc., 1971.

Campion, Nicholas. *The Book of World Horoscopes*. Wellingborough, Northamptonshire: Aquarian Press, 1988.

Carter, Charles E. O. *The Principles of Astrology*. London: Theosophical Society Publishing House, 1925.

Davison, R. C. *The Technique of Prediction*. Essex: L. N. Fowler & Co., Ltd., 1955.

DeLong, Sylvia. *The Art of Horary Astrology in Practice*. Tempe, AZ: American Federation of Astrologers, 1980.

———. *Guideposts to Mystical and Mundane Interpretations*. Tempe, AZ: American Federation of Astrologers, 1979.

DeVore, Nicholas. *Encyclopedia of Astrology*. New York: Philosophical Library, 1947.

Ebertin, Reinhold. *The Combination of Stellar Influences*. Tempe, AZ: American Federation of Astrologers, 1940.

Epstein, Alan. *Understanding Aspects: The Inconjunct*. Reno, NV: Trines Publishing, 1996.

Frawley, David. *The Astrology of Seers*. Salt Lake City, UT: Passage Press, 1990.

Goldstein-Jacobson, Ivy M. *All Over the Earth Astrologically*. Pasadena, CA: Pasadena Lithographers, 1963.

———. *Here and There in Astrology*. Pasadena, CA: Pasadena Lithographers, 1961.

———. *In the Beginning, Astrology*. Alhambra, CA: Frank Severy Publishing, 1975.

———. *Simplified Horary Astrology*. Alhambra, CA: Frank Severy Publishing, 1960.

Greene, Liz. *The Outer Planets and Their Cycles*. Reno, NV: CRCS Publications, 1983.

———. *Saturn: A New Look at an Old Devil*. New York: Samuel Weiser, Inc., 1976.

Hamaker-Zondag, Karen. *The Yod Book*. York Beach, ME: Samuel Weiser, Inc., 2000.

Hand, Robert. *Planets in Transit*. Rockport, MA: Para Research, 1976.

Hickey, Isabel M. *Astrology: A Cosmic Science*. Watertown, MA: Fellowship House, 1970.

Huber, Bruno, and Louise Huber. *Moon Node Astrology*. York Beach, ME: Samuel Weiser, Inc., 1995.

Jansky, Robert Carl. *Interpreting the Eclipses*. San Diego, CA: ACS Publications, 1979.

Jones, Marc Edmund. *A Guide to Horoscope Interpretation*. Wheaton, IL: Theosophical Publishing House, 1974.

———. *Problem Solving by Horary Astrology*. Philadelphia, PA: David McKay, 1946.

Lewis, James R. *The Astrology Encyclopedia*. Detroit, MI: Visible Ink Press, 1994.

Lineman, Rose. *Eclipse Interpretation Manual*. Tempe, AZ: American Federation of Astrologers, 1986.

Louis, Anthony. *Horary Astrology*. St. Paul, MN: Llewellyn Publications, 1991.

Lundsted, Betty. *Planetary Cycles*. York Beach, ME: Samuel Weiser, Inc., 1984.

March, Marion D., and Joan McEvers. *The Only Way to Learn Astrology, Volume I: Basic Principles*. San Diego, CA: ACS Publications, 1976.

———. *The Only Way to Learn Astrology, Volume II: Math & Interpretation Techniques*. San Diego, CA: ACS Publications, 1977.

———. *The Only Way to Learn Astrology, Volume III: Horoscope Analysis*. San Diego, CA: ACS Publications, 1982.

———. *The Only Way to Learn About Horary and Electional Astrology, Volume VI*. San Diego, CA: ACS Publications, 1994.

Mason, Sophia. *Delineation of Progressions*. Tempe, AZ: American Federation of Astrologers, 1985.

———. *Forecasting With New, Full and Quarter Moons*. Parma, OH:
Aquarian-Cancerian Publications, 1980.

———. *From One House to Another*. Parma, OH: Aquarian-Cancerian
Publications, 1977.

———. *Understanding Planetary Placements*. Parma, OH: Aquarian-Cancerian Publications, 1977.

McWhirter, Louise. *Astrology and Stock Market Forecasting*. Second edition. New York: ASI Publishers, Inc., 1977.

Merriman, Raymond A. *The New Solar Return Book of Prediction*. Bloom-
field, MI: Seek-It Publications, 1977.

Navarro, Gilbert. *Correspondence Course in Horary Astrology*. Edgewood,
MD: Gilbert Navarro, 1987.

———. *In Horary, Can an Astrologer Move Faster Than His Planets?* Tempe,
AZ: American Federation of Astrologers Bulletin, Volume 39, 1977.

Palmer, Lynne. *Gambling to Win*. Tempe, AZ: American Federation of
Astrologers, 1994.

Pelletier, Robert. *Planets in Aspect*. Rockport, MA: Para Research, 1974.

Ptolemy. *Tetrabiblos*. Trans. J. M. Ashmand. North Hollywood, CA:
Symbols and Signs, 1976.

Robson, Vivien E. *Electional Astrology*. New York: Samuel Weiser, Inc.,
1972.

Rudhyar, Dane. *Astrological Signs*. Boulder, CO: Shambhala Publications,
1978.

———. *The Lunation Cycle*. Boulder, CO: Shambhala Publications, 1971.

Sakoian, Frances, and Louis Acker. *The Astrologer's Handbook*. New York:
Harper & Row, 1973.

Shea, Mary. *Planets in Solar Returns*. San Diego, CA: ACS Publications, 1992.

Tyl, Noel. *Prediction in Astrology*. St Paul, MN: Llewellyn Publications, 1991.

————. *The Principles and Practice of Astrology, Volume IV*. St. Paul, MN: Llewellyn Publications, 1977.

Unger, Anne, and Lillian Huber. *The Horary Reference Book*. San Diego, CA: ACS Publications, 1984.

Watters, Barbara H. *Horary Astrology and the Judgement of Events*. Washington, DC: Valhalla Paperbacks, 1973.

Wehrman, Joyce C. *Winning*. LaMesa, CA: Wherman, 1980.

TO WRITE TO THE AUTHOR

If you wish to contact the author or would like more information about this book, please write to the author in care of Llewellyn Worldwide and we will forward your request. Both the author and publisher appreciate hearing from you and learning of your enjoyment of this book and how it has helped you. Llewellyn Worldwide cannot guarantee that every letter written to the author can be answered, but all will be forwarded. Please write to:

Joann Hampar
℅ Llewellyn Worldwide
P.O. Box 64383, Dept. 0-7387-0701-5
St. Paul, MN 55164-0383, U.S.A.

Please enclose a self-addressed stamped envelope for reply,
or $1.00 to cover costs. If outside U.S.A., enclose
international postal reply coupon.

Many of Llewellyn's authors have websites with additional information and resources.
For more information, please visit our website at
http://www.llewellyn.com

Free Magazine

Read unique articles by Llewellyn authors, recommendations by experts, and information on new releases. To receive a **free** copy of Llewellyn's consumer magazine, *New Worlds of Mind & Spirit,* simply call 1-877-NEW-WRLD or visit our website at www.llewellyn.com and click on *New Worlds.*

☾ LLEWELLYN ORDERING INFORMATION

Order Online:
Visit our website at www.llewellyn.com, select your books, and order them on our secure server.

Order by Phone:
- Call toll-free within the U.S. at 1-877-NEW-WRLD (1-877-639-9753). Call toll-free within Canada at 1-866-NEW-WRLD (1-866-639-9753).
- We accept VISA, MasterCard, and American Express

Order by Mail:
Send the full price of your order (MN residents add 7% sales tax) in U.S. funds, plus postage & handling to:

> **Llewellyn Worldwide**
> **P.O. Box 64383, Dept. 0-7387-00701-5**
> **St. Paul, MN 55164-0383, U.S.A.**

Postage & Handling:

Standard (U.S., Mexico, & Canada). If your order is:
> $49.99 and under, add $3.00
> $50.00 and over, FREE STANDARD SHIPPING

AK, HI, PR: $15.00 for one book plus $1.00 for each additional book.

International Orders (airmail only):
> $16.00 for one book plus $3.00 for each additional book

Orders are processed within 2 business days.
Please allow for normal shipping time. Postage and handling rates subject to change.

The New A to Z Horoscope Maker and Delineator

LLEWELLYN GEORGE

A textbook . . . encyclopedia . . . self-study course . . . and extensive astrological dictionary all in one! More American astrologers have learned their craft from *The New A to Z Horoscope and Delineator* than any other astrology book.

First published in 1910, it is in every sense a complete course in astrology, giving beginners all the basic techniques and concepts they need to get off on the right foot. Plus it offers the more advanced astrologer an excellent dictionary and reference work for calculating and analyzing transits, progression, rectifications, and creating locality charts. This new edition has been revised to meet the needs of the modern audience.

0-7387-322-2, 480 pp., 7½ x 9⅛   **$19.95**

Llewellyn's Astrology Datebook
2006 Daily Planetary Guide

Moon Sign & Phase, Weekly Forecasts for Everyone, & Daily Aspectarian.

More than a datebook, the *Daily Planetary Guide* is a powerhouse of planetary insight. It has all the day-to-day astrological information anyone could want between two covers. Knowing when to schedule a long-awaited vacation or ask for that much-deserved raise is made a whole lot easier when you tap into the powerful energies that affect you every day.

This year's edition features Opportunity Periods— times when the positive flow of energy won't be obstructed by transiting planets. From closing a business deal to searching for romance, astrologer Jim Shawvan also explains how to take advantage of these special times.

0-7387-0155-6, spiral-bound datebook, 208 pp., 5¼ x 8, ephemerides $9.99

The Art of
Predictive Astrology
Forecasting Your Life Events

Carol Rushman

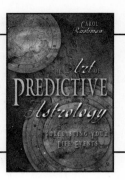

Become an expert at seeing the future in anyone's astrological chart! Insight into the future is a large part of the intrigue and mystery of astrology. *The Art of Predictive Astrology* clearly lays out a step-by-step system that astrologers can use to forecast significant events including love and financial success. When finished with the book, readers will be able to predict cycles and trends for the next several years, and give their clients fifteen important dates for the coming year. An emphasis is on progressions, eclipses, and lunations as important predictive tools.

0-7387-0164-5, 288 pp., 6 x 9 $14.95

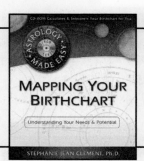

Mapping Your Birthchart
Understanding Your Needs & Potential

STEPHANIE JEAN CLEMENT, PH.D.

You know your "sign," but that's just the tip of the astrological iceberg. You've got a moon sign, a rising sign, and loads of other factors in your astrological makeup. Together they form the complete picture of you as an individual: your desires, talents, emotions . . . and your public persona and your private needs.

Mapping Your Birthchart removes the mystery from astrology so you can look at any chart and get a basic understanding of the person behind it. Learn the importance of the planets, the different signs of the zodiac, and how they relate to your everyday life. Stephanie Jean Clement introduces the basics of the astrology chart, devotes a chapter to each planet—with information about signs, houses, and aspects—provides simple explanations of astrological and psychological factors, and includes examples from the charts of well-known people including Tiger Woods, Celine Dion, and George W. Bush.

The free CD-ROM included with this book allows you to calculate and interpret your birthchart, and print out astrological reports and charts for yourself, your family, and friends.

Check out the other books in the series:
- *Mapping Your Future*
- *Mapping Your Money*
- *Mapping Your Family Relationships*
- *Mapping Your Romantic Relationships*

0-7387-0202-1, 240 pp., 7½ x 9¾, includes CD-ROM $19.95

SW

click. click. click.

- ⊙ **online bookstore**
- ⊙ **free web tarot**